DISEASES & DISORDERS

Growth Disorders

Lizabeth Peak

LUCENT BOOKS

An imprint of Thomson Gale, a part of The Thomson Corporation

THOMSON

GALE™

Detroit • London

For more information, contact
Lucent Books
27500 Drake Rd.
Farmington Hills, MI 48331-3535
Or you can visit our Internet site at http://www.gale.com

Picture Credits:
Cover: Gstar; AP Images, 46, 59, 70, 73; © Bettmann/CORBIS, 10, 27, 62; © CORBIS, 22; © Laura Dwight/CORBIS, 36; © Michael Keller/CORBIS, 7; © Lester Lefkowitz/CORBIS, 38; © Jose Luis Pelaez/CORBIS, 37; © Chris Stewart/*San Francisco Chronicle*/CORBIS, 79; Stone/Getty Images, 14; Kaosiung Chang Gung Hospital/AFP/Getty Images, 48; © BISP/Kretz Technik/Photo Researchers, Inc., 31; Neil Borden/Photo Researchers, Inc., 45, 77; Scott Camazine/Photo Researchers, Inc., 18, 34; David Fraser/Photo Researchers, Inc., 63; Clive Freeman/Photo Researchers, Inc., 13; Sam Ogden/ Photo Researchers, Inc., 76; Garo/Phanie/Photo Researchers, Inc., 66; John Radcliffe Hospital/ Photo Researchers, Inc., 19; Saturn Stills/ Photo Researchers, Inc., 33; SPL/Photo Researchers, Inc.ephyr/Photo Researchers, Inc., 49; Thomson-Gale, 21, 43

LIBRARY OF CONGRESS CATALOGING-IN-PUBLICATION DATA

Peak, Lizabeth.
  Growth disorders / by Lizabeth Peak.
    p. cm. — (Diseases and disorders)
  Includes bibliographical references and index.
  ISBN 978-1-59018-673-2 (hardcover)
  1. Growth disorders—Juvenile literature. I. Title.
  RJ482.G76P43 2007
  618.92'4—dc22

                                    2007007803

ISBN-10: 1-59018-673-7

Printed in the United States of America

Table of Contents

"The Most Difficult Puzzles Ever Devised"

Charles Best, one of the pioneers in the search for a cure for diabetes, once explained what it is about medical research that intrigued him so. "It's not just the gratification of knowing one is helping people," he confided, "although that probably is a more heroic and selfless motivation. Those feelings may enter in, but truly, what I find best is the feeling of going toe to toe with nature, of trying to solve the most difficult puzzles ever devised. The answers are there somewhere, those keys that will solve the puzzle and make the patient well. But how will those keys be found?"

Since the dawn of civilization, nothing has so puzzled people—and often frightened them, as well—as the onset of illness in a body or mind that had seemed healthy before. A seizure, the inability of a heart to pump, the sudden deterioration of muscle tone in a small child—being unable to reverse such conditions or even to understand why they occur was unspeakably frustrating to healers. Even before there were names for such conditions, even before they were understood at all, each was a reminder of how complex the human body was, and how vulnerable.

While our grappling with understanding diseases has been frustrating at times, it has also provided some of humankind's most heroic accomplishments. Alexander Fleming's accidental discovery in 1928 of a mold that could be turned into penicillin has resulted in the saving of untold millions of lives. The isolation of the enzyme insulin has reversed what was once a death sentence for anyone with diabetes. There have been great strides in combating conditions for which there is not yet a cure, too. Medicines can help AIDS patients live longer, diagnostic tools such as mammography and ultrasounds can help doctors find tumors while they are treatable, and laser surgery techniques have made the most intricate, minute operations routine.

This "toe-to-toe" competition with diseases and disorders is even more remarkable when seen in a historical continuum. An astonishing amount of progress has been made in a very short time. Just two hundred years ago, the existence of germs as a cause of some diseases was unknown. In fact, it was less than 150 years ago that a British surgeon named Joseph Lister had difficulty persuading his fellow doctors that washing their hands before delivering a baby might increase the chances of a healthy delivery (especially if they had just attended to a diseased patient)!

Each book in Lucent's Diseases and Disorders series explores a disease or disorder and the knowledge that has been accumulated (or discarded) by doctors through the years. Each book also examines the tools used for pinpointing a diagnosis, as well as the various means that are used to treat or cure a disease. Finally, new ideas are presented—techniques or medicines that may be on the horizon.

Frustration and disappointment are still part of medicine, for not every disease or condition can be cured or prevented. But the limitations of knowledge are being pushed outward constantly; the "most difficult puzzles ever devised" are finding challengers every day.

The Importance of Height

A young mother worries because her three-year-old son is the shortest child in his preschool class. Another mother brings her thirteen-year-old daughter to the doctor because she is already almost 6 feet tall (1.82m) and is being teased by her classmates. She wonders if there is any way to make her daughter stop growing. A newlywed couple is concerned about having children because the wife's older sister has a child who is a dwarf. They want to know if it runs in families. "Size is always a concern for families," says one physician. "As pediatricians, we are regularly confronted by parents who are worried about their children's height."[1]

A Common Occurrence

It is estimated that approximately 2 million children in the United States are affected by some kind of short stature; about five hundred thousand of them have severe growth problems. According to the Human Growth Foundation, approximately thirteen thousand children in the United States are affected by growth hormone deficiency. Another twenty thousand are affected by excessive tallness. Growth disorders affect boys and girls, men and women, of all races and socioeconomic levels. Growth disorders result from a wide range of causes. They can be genetic in nature, either passed on from parents or the result of a spontaneous mutation in a gene. They may be caused by problems with the endocrine glands or with other body systems. They can even be caused by long-term neglect and abuse.

The Need for Education

Growth disorders are often misunderstood by society. Contrary to popular beliefs, most short-statured individuals have a normal life span and normal intelligence. However, much of what most

A doctor measures a child's height. Pediatricians often encounter parents who are worried about their child's height.

people believe about short people, dwarfs in particular, has come from movies, television, and shows such as circuses, which tend to portray dwarfs as oddities. In mythology, dwarfs have often been incorrectly considered to be an entirely different species from "normal" humans and are portrayed in a negative light. To address this lack of understanding, many organizations such as Little People of America, the Human Growth Foundation, and the MAGIC Foundation provide education for the public, awareness of what growth disorders are, and support for research into growth disorders.

Dr. Tom Shakespeare, a genetics expert at Newcastle University in England, has spent much of his life studying the science behind dwarfism. Shakespeare, who has achondroplasia, is currently conducting a research project that he hopes will change people's attitudes toward dwarfism. "We're hoping to understand more about the medical and social problems that people with restricted growth face," says Shakespeare. "There's still a lot of ignorance about dwarfism."[2]

How Short Is "Too Short?"

Physicians consider a child to be excessively short if he or she is shorter than 97 percent of children of the same age and sex. Little People of America, an organization created for little people and their families both in the United States and around the world, defines dwarfism as an adult height less than 4 feet 10 inches (1.47m) for both men and women.

There are two broad categories of dwarfism. Disproportionate short stature means that the arms and legs are much shorter in proportion to an average-sized head and trunk. This is the type of short stature seen in conditions such as achondroplasia and other skeletal disorders in which the bones of the limbs, hands, and feet do not grow properly. Proportionate dwarfism, also sometimes called pituitary dwarfism, means that the arms, legs, head, and trunk are all in normal proportion to one another. People with proportionate dwarfism look the same as average-size people—they are just extremely short. They were once referred to as midgets, but this term has fallen out of favor. The term is now offensive to many little people, which is the preferred term for both kinds of dwarfism. Ivy, a British teenager with dwarfism, explains about what to call a small person. "This is a tricky one, and there's no right answer. I am comfortable with the word dwarf, but because of the negative way in which it has been used, many people aren't. The entirely PC [politically correct] term would be 'a person of restricted growth,' but most would be comfortable with 'little person,' or small short person. It is important to remember that while we may look unusual, we are not a different species: 'it' is not an acceptable pronoun."[3]

Heightism

There are many more issues for short-statured people to deal with other than terminology. Society places a great deal of importance on a person's height. From infancy, a person's size is noted with comments such as "My, how you've grown!" and "Eat all your vegetables so you'll grow big." Children who are shorter than most of their peers become especially aware of their height when they start school. "By elementary school, children start noticing differences in height—and kids who don't measure up begin to hear about it,"[4] says one psychology professor. Throughout their school years, short children, especially boys, must contend with teasing and bullying. They are often seen as weaker and less able to defend themselves.

In adulthood, short people often feel discriminated against. They point out examples such as the fact that in all but three presidential elections in the twentieth century, the taller candidate has won. A survey done in 1980 found that more than half of the chief executives of America's Fortune 500 companies were 6 feet tall (1.82m) or taller. Another study found that people in high-ranking jobs were on average about 2 inches (5cm) taller than those in lower-ranking jobs. Still other studies have shown that taller people, both men and women, tend to earn more money than shorter people. Finally, short men feel at a disadvantage when it comes to dating and finding a marriage partner. In another 1980 survey, by Ralph Keyes, only two out

Charles Stratton, a little person who came to be known as Tom Thumb, was P.T. Barnum's first major circus attraction. Many incorrect beliefs about short people come from movies, television, and circuses.

of seventy-nine women said they would go on a date with a man who was shorter than they were.

A More Positive Outlook

Despite these examples of discrimination, there is significant evidence to support the opposite case. In 1998 researchers at the University of Buffalo in New York compared the quality of life of adults who had been treated for short stature as children with their siblings who had grown normally. The study found that the former patients were just as happy and satisfied with their lives as their healthy brothers and sisters. Another study published in 2004 in the medical journal *Pediatrics* showed that kids' height, whether extra short or extra tall, had no effect on their popularity. The study was set up to determine whether kids preferred taller classmates as friends and whether shorter kids were left out of activities. "What we found reflects the folk wisdom that it's what's inside that counts," said the lead author of the study. "Being a good friend is going to determine how well you're liked, more than how tall you are."[5]

CHAPTER ONE

What Are Growth Disorders?

A growth disorder is any disorder that causes a child's rate of growth to be much slower or much faster than established standards of normal growth. Factors such as genetics, hormones, other diseases, and one's environment all influence how people grow. Growth disorders can occur because of problems with any of these influences. Some, such as achondroplasia (a form of dwarfism) and Marfan syndrome (which causes excessive growth), are genetic in nature, either the result of a mutation that occurs at conception or the result of a faulty gene that gets passed down from one or both parents. Other growth disorders, such as growth hormone deficiency and hypothyroidism, occur when the body produces inadequate amounts of the hormones necessary for normal growth or when the body does not respond to these hormones properly. Diseases involving other body systems, particularly kidney or intestinal diseases, often have a significant effect on growth. Environmental issues, especially malnutrition in the mother or the child or stress from severe neglect or abuse, can also cause problems with growth.

The Gift of Heredity

Of all the factors determining how a person grows, one of the most important is heredity—the characteristics that are passed on to a child from his or her parents. Children's growth tends to mirror that of their parents—short parents often have short children, and tall parents tend to have tall children. Their height characteristics are familial, meaning that they do not necessarily have a growth disorder; their height runs in their family. Because these inherited growth patterns are considered normal variations of growth and do not cause other problems, they are rarely treated. At nineteen years of age, Louise stood just under 5 feet (1.52m) tall. "My height never really bothered me when I was a young child," says Louise, "which was probably because no one made an issue of it. I remember when I was 10 1/2, I was referred to the hospital for my height. I had X-rays and blood tests done for about a year and a half but they found nothing wrong. They just put it down to genes."[6] Genetic growth problems, however, can cause significant challenges for those who are affected. The secret is locked inside submicroscopic particles called genes.

A Secret Code

Genes are extremely tiny chemical units that children inherit from their parents at conception. Genes are made up of a chemical called deoxyribonucleic acid, or DNA. DNA carries encoded within it all the information that the body's cells need

DNA carries the information that determines cell development and function.

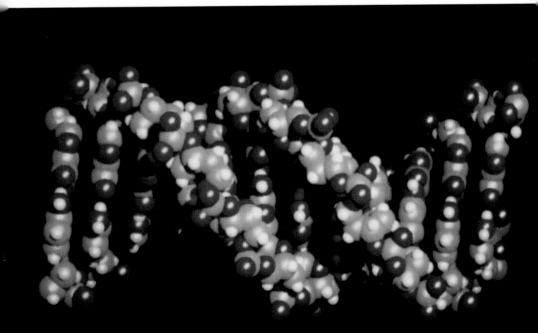

in order to know what kind of cells they are to become and what their function will be. DNA is made up of four chemicals, called bases, which are abbreviated A, T, C, and G. The bases are paired with each other in a specific sequence along the genes. This sequence is extremely important because it determines what kind of organism will be built, whether human, insect, or bacteria.

Human chromosomes are found in the nucleus of every living cell.

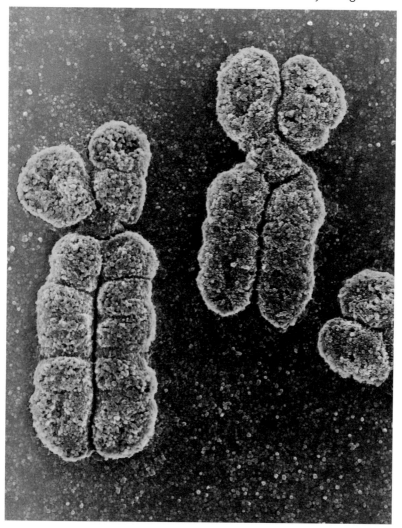

Genes are arranged along threadlike structures called chromosomes, which are found in the nucleus of every living cell. Each chromosome carries on it approximately 140,000 genes. Human beings have forty-six chromosomes in each cell nucleus, twenty-three received from each parent. Forty-four of the chromosomes are organized into twenty-two pairs. The other two are unpaired sex chromosomes, called X and Y. Girls have two X chromosomes; boys have one X and one Y. Every human trait is determined at conception by the genes that are inherited from parents. Whether children show a trait given to them from their father or from their mother depends on whether the gene is dominant or recessive.

Dominant and Recessive Genes

If a gene is dominant, it means that the trait for that gene will always show, even if only one parent passes the gene to the child. If a gene is recessive, both parents must pass on the gene in order for the trait to show. If one parent has one dominant gene, there is a 50 percent chance that the child will show the trait. If both parents have one, there is a 75 percent chance that their child will show it. A simple example of this is eye color. The gene for brown eyes is dominant; the one for blue eyes is recessive. In order for a person to have blue eyes, he or she must inherit two genes for blue eyes. If he or she inherits even one brown-eye gene, he or she will have brown eyes. If a mutation, or change, occurs in a dominant gene, or if a child inherits a mutant recessive gene from both parents, the child will show the trait as it is affected by the mutation.

Genetic Mutation

Mutations are changes that occur in the DNA of genes. Mutations can happen because of damage to the genes caused by drug or alcohol use by the mother; some illnesses, such as rubella; and advanced age of the mother or father. Many times, the cause of the mutation cannot be known.

Genetic mutations can happen in several different ways. Sometimes, a section of DNA in a gene becomes detached from the chromosome and is lost. Turner syndrome, for example, which causes short stature in girls, occurs when an X chromosome is partially or completely missing. Sometimes a section can be duplicated and appear twice on the chromosome. Sometimes a section can be attached backward or become attached to the wrong chromosome. Depending on the gene affected, some mutations can cause the child to die before or shortly after birth. Fortunately, though, the great majority of genetic mutations cause little or no harm, because they occur in a recessive gene rather than a dominant one.

Achondroplasia

Achondroplasia is an example of a genetic mutation that occurs in a dominant gene. The word *achondroplasia* comes from Greek and means "without cartilage formation" (although people with the condition do have cartilage). It is the most common of the more than two hundred different types of skeletal dysplasias, or disorders of bone growth, occurring in one in every twenty-six thousand to forty thousand births. Children with achondroplasia grow to be only about 4 feet tall (1.22m), with a normal-sized head and torso but very short arms and legs. This is because cartilage cells in the long bones of the unborn child's arms and legs do not turn into bone properly. Because of the mutation, these cells receive faulty information about what they are supposed to do.

Cameron, a very active and outgoing six-year-old, was born with achondroplasia. When Cameron was born, says his mother Dina, "One of the nurses said, 'If the doctors say he has skeletal dysplasia, it's just another word for dwarfism.'"[7] Six hours later, Cameron's parents were visited by a geneticist, a doctor who specializes in genetic disorders. He told them that Cameron had achondroplasia. His mother's thoughts immediately went to his future. "I just instantly thought, what does this mean for his life? I jumped way ahead of a baby's needs to junior high, high school, girlfriends. I just way jumped the gun."[8]

The great majority of cases of achondroplasia, about 75 to 80 percent, are in children born to average-sized parents. In these

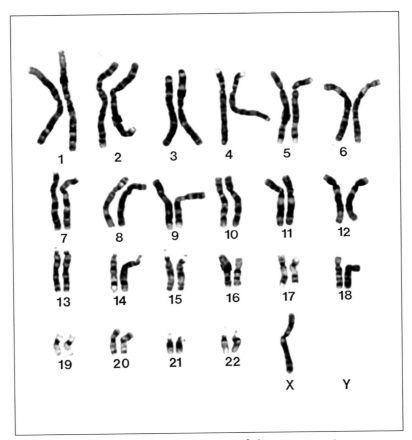

This micrograph shows the arrangement of chromosomes in a woman with Turner syndrome. The second X chromosome is missing, resulting in stunted growth.

cases, the condition is not inherited but is caused by a spontaneous mutation that occurs at conception. Genetic scientists do not know why the mutation occurs, although they have noted that fathers over forty years of age are more likely than younger fathers to have children with achondroplasia. In about 25 percent of cases, the child inherits the condition from a parent who already has it. If both parents have achondroplasia, and the child inherits the faulty gene from both parents, a condition called double dominant syndrome occurs. The resulting skeletal abnormalities are so severe that the child will die soon after birth.

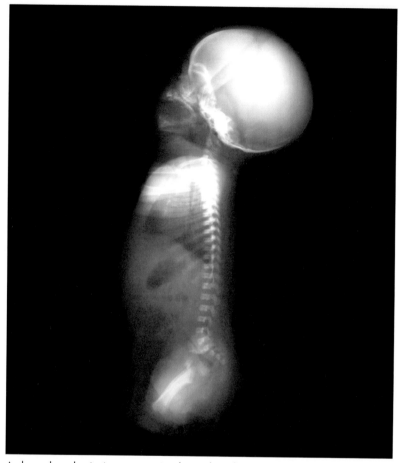

Achondroplasia is a genetic disorder that is evident at birth and is characterized by abnormal body proportions.

Marfan Syndrome

Marfan syndrome is another genetic disorder that, unlike achondroplasia, causes excessive growth. Marfan syndrome affects the connective tissue of the body, which acts to hold the body and its various organs together. Connective tissue is found throughout the body, so Marfan syndrome affects many different systems, especially the skeleton, eyes, heart, blood vessels, nervous system, skin, and lungs. Some people with Marfan syndrome have many symptoms; others have fewer. Most affected people are very tall and slender with a long, narrow face and long, loose-jointed arms and legs. Their chest may have a caved-in look due to curvature of the breastbone.

The most severe potential complications of Marfan syndrome involve the heart and large blood vessels. The valves in the heart may leak because they do not close properly. Weakened connective tissue can cause a weakened aorta, the large artery that leads out of the heart. The pressure of the blood passing through the aorta can cause it to thin out and expand, like a balloon filling with air. If the aorta breaks, or ruptures, it is a life-threatening emergency.

Genetic Mutations and Hormones

Genetic mutations can also cause malfunctions in the body's production and response to hormones. Hormones are chemical substances that are produced by special organs called endocrine glands. Each type of endocrine gland produces its own kinds of hormones and secretes them into the bloodstream, where they travel to their genetically programmed target organ. The hormone then acts like a messenger by giving the organ instructions about what it is supposed to do.

The hands on the left are the hands of a person with Marfan syndrome, showing abnormally long, slender fingers. The hand on the right is a normal-sized hand.

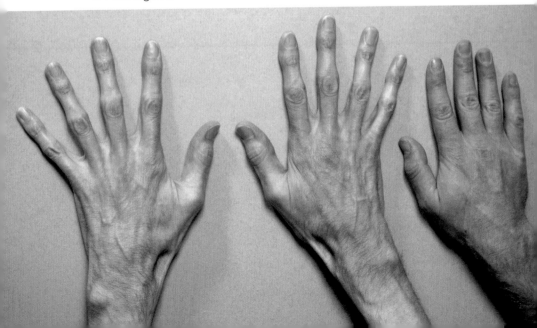

There are more than twenty major hormones produced by the endocrine glands. Several of these have a direct effect on growth. Some, such as growth hormone, act directly on their target organs. Others, such as thyroid-stimulating hormone, are called trophic hormones. They act by triggering the release of hormones from other glands. Trophic hormones can regulate themselves through a system called biofeedback. As one researcher explains: "A trophic hormone speeds up production of its target gland. Then, some of the hormones . . . send a message back to the pituitary to slow down its production of the trophic hormone. It's like the thermostat that controls your furnace and keeps the house temperature constant."[9] Any problem that causes too much or too little of these hormones to be produced will result in a growth disorder. Controlling the release of hormones by the endocrine glands is the responsibility of the pituitary gland.

The Master Gland

The pituitary gland is a pea-sized gland located deep inside the skull at the base of the brain. It is often called the master gland because it makes the trophic hormones that control several of the other glands. The pituitary itself is controlled by a part of the brain called the hypothalamus, which secretes its own hormones that control the activities of the pituitary. The pituitary gland is divided into two halves—the anterior, or front, lobe, and the posterior, or back, lobe. The anterior lobe has the most control over growth by secreting several hormones that are critical for normal growth.

Growth Hormone and IGF-1

Growth hormone, secreted by the anterior lobe of the pituitary gland in response to instructions from the hypothalamus, stimulates the growth of body tissues such as bone, muscle, fat, and internal organs. It also helps maintain the proper balance of muscle and fat by controlling how the body uses nutrients such as protein, sugar, and fat, and minerals such as calcium. When growth hormone is secreted into the bloodstream, it stimulates

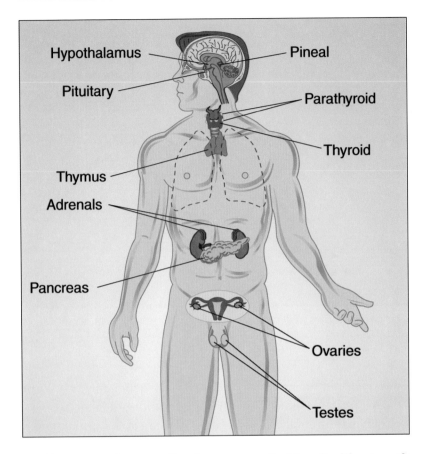

Hypothalamus

Pineal

Pituitary

Parathyroid

Thyroid

Thymus

Adrenals

Pancreas

Ovaries

Testes

the liver to produce another hormone called insulin-like growth factor 1, or IGF-1. One of the several functions of IGF-1 is to stimulate bone and tissue growth. When the amount of IGF-1 reaches its proper level, it then signals the pituitary to reduce its production of growth hormone. In this way, a proper balance of both of these hormones is maintained.

Not Enough Hormone

When the pituitary gland fails to produce enough growth hormone, or when the body's tissues do not respond to it properly, growth is impaired. It is estimated that ten thousand to fifteen thousand children in the United States have growth failure caused by growth hormone deficiency. Children with growth hormone deficiency grow much slower and are much shorter than

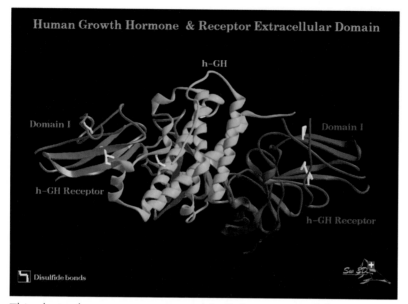

This photo shows a computer model of a human growth hormone molecule and its receptors. Growth hormone is secreted by the pituitary gland and stimulates the growth of body tissues.

other children their age. Growth hormone deficiency can occur by itself or in combination with other hormone deficiencies.

There are several possible causes for growth hormone deficiency. Sometimes the pituitary gland or the hypothalamus do not form properly before birth. There can be damage to these structures from a lack of oxygen during the birth process. Head injuries, brain surgery, or severe illnesses such as meningitis or encephalitis, which cause inflammation of the brain and surrounding tissues, can also damage them. Some cases are caused by a tumor called a craniopharyngioma. This tumor can press on the pituitary or the hypothalamus, causing them to malfunction and produce inadequate amounts of their hormones.

When growth hormone is inadequate, it often leads to a deficiency in IGF-1. Until recently, many children who were very short but had normal levels of growth hormone were classified as having idiopathic (of unknown cause) short stature. This means that there was no apparent cause for their growth failure. In 2005 researchers discovered that as many as thirty thousand children in the United States may have a deficiency of IGF-1, even though their growth hormone level is normal. This is called primary IGF-1 deficiency (IGFD). The researchers found that primary IGFD is about as common as growth hormone deficiency. They estimate that one-third to one-half of idiopathic short stature children can now be diagnosed with and treated for primary IGFD. One of the study's authors explains, "We now know . . . that IGF-1 deficiency is much more than an indicator of growth hormone deficiency and should be considered as a distinct diagnostic category."[10]

Too Much Hormone

Growth disorders involving abnormally tall stature are much less common than those causing short stature. In almost all cases of abnormal extreme height, the cause is an overproduction of growth hormone by the pituitary. Traditionally, this condition has been called pituitary gigantism or giantism, although there is no established definition of how tall a person has to be to be called a giant. The most common cause for this overproduction is a tumor on the pituitary gland called a pituitary adenoma, an abnormal growth of cells in the gland that do not respond to the control of the hypothalamus.

Besides extreme tallness, children with pituitary gigantism have heavy, thick bones, with large hands and feet and a heavy jaw. Because the internal organs are also affected, the chest and abdomen may also look larger than normal. The condition can cause a delay in the onset of puberty. If the condition is not treated, and the excessive growth hormone production continues after bone growth has stopped in the teen years, the condition is called acromegaly. Acromegaly can also begin later in life, after a childhood of normal growth, if the affected person develops a pituitary adenoma as an adult.

Acromegaly is not very common; scientists estimate that three out of every 1 million people develop the disease every year. However, because the symptoms of acromegaly often develop slowly over time, many people do not even realize they have the disease until it is far advanced. Adults with acromegaly develop large hands and feet, thick fingers, and heavy facial features. Other symptoms include coarse, oily skin; enlarged lips, nose, and tongue; fatigue and weakness; and enlargement of other body organs. If the disease is not treated, it can lead to more serious symptoms such as arthritis, headaches, vision problems, diabetes, high blood pressure, and heart disease.

Other Hormones and Growth

Besides controlling the release of growth hormone, the pituitary also balances the amounts of hormones produced by other glands. Certain other hormones produced in the anterior pituitary perform this function. An imbalance in any of them can lead to growth failure. Thyroid-stimulating hormone stimulates the thyroid gland, located in the front of the neck, to secrete thyroid hormone. An inadequate supply of thyroid-stimulating hormone causes a condition called hypothyroidism, which leads to an inadequate supply of thyroid hormone. Hypothyroidism can also be caused by problems within the thyroid gland itself. Cells respond to thyroid hormone by increasing their metabolic rate, which is the process that produces energy and the chemicals necessary for cells to grow and divide. Without enough thyroid hormone, this process slows down, so growth slows down. Often, failure to grow is one of the first signs of hypothyroidism. Left untreated, hypothyroidism in newborns can cause irreversible mental retardation and other developmental delays.

An overproduction of cortisol, a hormone produced by the adrenal glands in response to instructions from the pituitary, can cause the hormonal imbalance called Cushing's syndrome. The most common cause of Cushing's syndrome is a pituitary adenoma that secretes too much of the hormone ACTH, which acts on the adrenal glands. It can also be caused by tumors in the adrenals or in other parts of the body that can secrete ACTH. Cortisol has many important functions. Its roles in growth include balancing the effect of insulin in breaking down sugars for energy and regulating the metabolism of protein, fats, and carbohydrates. In growing children, too much cortisol in the blood can cause weight gain and growth retardation.

The anterior pituitary secretes two hormones that have their greatest effect in the teen years. Luteinizing hormone and follicle-stimulating hormone both stimulate the ovaries to produce estrogen and progesterone in girls, and stimulate the testes to produce testosterone in boys. These hormones are responsible for the adolescent growth spurt and for the proper development

This man suffers from acromegaly. The condition causes uncontrolled growth leading to elongated, heavy facial features and large hands and feet.

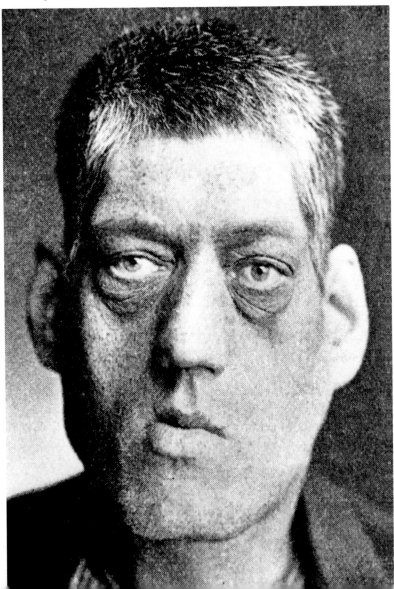

Robert Wadlow— the Gentle Giant

Robert Pershing Wadlow is the tallest human for whom there is actual documentation. When he died at age twenty-two, he was 8 feet 11 inches tall (2.72m) and weighed 490 pounds (222kg). It is believed that he was still growing just before he died.

Robert was born in Alton, Illinois, in 1918. He weighed 8 pounds (3.6kg) and was normal length. He grew normally until he was about four years old, when he began growing very rapidly. By eight years old, he was 6 feet 2 inches (1.88m). At ten, he was 6 feet 6 inches (1.98m). When he was fourteen, he became the world's tallest Boy Scout, at 7 feet 4 inches (2.24m) and wore a size 25 shoe. By the time he was nineteen years old, he had grown to be 8 feet 6 inches (2.59m) and weighed 435 pounds (197kg).

Robert's size took a toll on his body. He needed leg braces to walk and had little feeling in his legs and feet. On the Fourth of July, 1940,

---

of adult sexual characteristics. Estrogen (in both sexes) also signals the bones to stop growing as soon as they reach their genetically-determined adult length. A deficiency in any of these hormones causes a delay in the growth spurt and in sexual development.

Diseases of Body Systems

In addition to genetic causes and hormonal imbalances, several diseases that affect other body systems can cause short stature and growth failure if they are severe or untreated. Kidney disease, in particular, can have a profound effect on a child's growth. Besides cleaning waste products and extra fluid from the bloodstream, the kidneys also help regulate the amounts of nutrients in the body and how they are used. Calcium, phosphorus, and vitamin D are three nutrients that must be in balance in

Robert was hospitalized with a blister on his ankle which had become badly infected. Despite blood transfusions and surgery, Robert died from the infection.

Robert had a tumor on his pituitary gland that secreted large amounts of growth hormone. At the time Robert lived, methods of diagnosis and treatment of growth disorders was limited, and there was no therapy available for him. Today, Robert Wadlow is remembered as a quiet young man who overcame an enormous handicap. He is known in his hometown as the Gentle Giant.

Robert Wadlow stands next to two average-sized women.

order for bones to grow properly. The kidneys activate vitamin D, which is necessary for proper absorption of calcium from food. Malfunctioning kidneys also let too much phosphorus build up in the blood. When this happens, calcium cannot get into the bones, and they cannot grow normally. For this reason, children in renal failure, or failure of the kidneys to function properly, are often much shorter than their peers.

Several intestinal disorders can also cause short stature and growth failure because they prevent nutrients from being absorbed from food. Without proper absorption of nutrients, growth failure results. Celiac disease, an inability to tolerate gluten, a protein found in certain grains, causes damage to the lining of the intestines, resulting in poor absorption and growth failure. Crohn's disease is an inflammation of the small intestine that causes abdominal pain and rapid emptying of the intestine.

Crohn's disease, like celiac disease, prevents proper absorption of nutrients, leading to growth failure.

The liver is another major organ that must be healthy in order for normal growth to occur. In addition to its job of producing the growth hormone IGF-1, the liver is also responsible for storing extra vitamins, minerals, and sugar to help prevent shortages of these nutrients. It also helps to regulate the body's metabolism. Liver diseases such as biliary atresia and neonatal

What Are Growing Pains?

Sometimes during growth spurts, kids experience episodes of achy leg pains that almost always happen at night and disappear by morning. These are often called growing pains.

No one knows for sure what causes growing pains or why they only seem to happen at night. Dr. Thomas Lehman provides a possible reason: "There is evidence that the body produces more growth hormone at night, and some doctors believe the body is actually growing faster at night, leading to the pain." Adds Dr. Allan Greene, "The muscles and tendons are still a little too tight for the growing long bones. Muscle spasms lasting one to fifteen minutes cause the pain."

Most of the time, a little gentle massage to the sore joint, along with a warm, moist cloth, helps relieve the pain. Gentle upward stretching of the foot and toes can also help. If these things do not work, or if the pains are more severe, a dose of ibuprofen or acetaminophen can help. Daily stretching exercises to make muscles more flexible can help prevent the pains from coming back during the child's next growth spurt.

"Does Your Child Have Growing Pains?," by Dr. Thomas Lehman, 2004. www.goldscout.com/gpl.html.

"Growing Pains," by Dr. Alan Greene, 1996. www.drgreene.org/blank.cfm?print=yes+id=21&action=detail&ref=122.

hepatitis, which can destroy liver tissue, not only cause growth failure, but are also life threatening.

Environmental Factors

A fourth major factor affecting growth is the environment into which a child is born and lives. Human beings are influenced by their environment from the moment of conception, especially when it comes to growth. Studies have shown that women who smoke, drink alcohol, or use certain drugs during pregnancy risk having babies whose growth is stunted. Malnutrition and chronic, severe stress also play a particularly important role in growth problems.

Worldwide, poor nutrition is the single most common cause of growth failure in children. Inadequate nutrition in a pregnant woman can lead to a condition called intrauterine growth retardation, in which the baby does not grow well in the uterus because there is a lack of the nutrients needed for healthy growth. After birth, a balanced diet rich in protein, fats, vitamins, and minerals is essential for proper growth. Without proper nutrition, infants and young children will show a slower-than-expected weight and height gain, a condition known as failure to thrive. Fortunately, in most cases, normal growth will resume if adequate nutrition is eventually provided. International organizations such as the Peace Corps, UNICEF, the World Health Organization, and many others work to reduce or eliminate the harmful effects of malnutrition for children worldwide.

An environment high in stress can lead to slow or even halted growth in children. Studies have shown that when a child lives with constant stress from physical or emotional abuse or severe neglect, the body may actually slow or stop production of growth hormone. This condition is sometimes referred to as psychosocial short stature, or psychogenic dwarfism. The only treatment for this is to remove the child from the stressful environment and place him or her in a healthy, nurturing environment. If this is done, the child will begin to grow normally again. If the child is then returned to the stressful environment, his or her growth will slow once again.

CHAPTER TWO

Diagnosing Growth Disorders

The diagnosis of a growth disorder can begin even before a child is born. If there is a family history of a particular disorder, there are prenatal (before birth) tests that can be done to help determine whether or not the child will be born with the disorder. Ultrasound and genetic testing are two methods of diagnosing growth disorders before birth.

Ultrasound

Ultrasound, or sonography, is a test that uses very high frequency sound waves and their echoes to create a picture of internal tissues and organs. It works in a similar way to the echolocation used by bats, whales, and dolphins, and to the sonar devices aboard ships and submarines. To do this test, an ultrasound probe, which sends out the sound waves, is held gently against the skin. The frequency of the sound waves is much too high to be heard or felt. The sound waves echo off the internal tissues differently, depending on the density of the tissue. Soft tissues, fluid, and bone all echo the sound waves back to the probe in different ways.

The reflected waves are then sent to a computer, which turns the echoes into a two-dimensional picture, called a sonogram, on the screen. Even small details of a baby's development in the womb, such as the beating of its heart or the structures inside its brain, can be detected by the ultrasound. Recently, three-dimensional ultrasound has been developed that uses several probes to combine several two-dimensional scans into a much more detailed and accurate image. Whereas a two-dimensional sonogram resembles an X-ray, a three-dimensional image looks very much like a sculpture.

Ultrasound is particularly useful for detecting the presence of skeletal dysplasias. Skeletal dysplasias are growth disorders of the bones and cartilage. They may involve abnormal growth of the arms and legs, absence of all or part of a limb, or extra fingers and toes. There are over 175 different types of skeletal dysplasias, most of which are the result of genetic mutations. Achondroplasia is an example of a skeletal dysplasia. Dina, mother of six-year-old Cameron, remembers: "At the first ultrasound, at twenty weeks, they noticed he had club foot. They did ultrasounds every four weeks and at the second one, they noticed that his limbs were shorter." [11]

A 3-D ultrasound shows a scan of a thirty-week-old fetus.

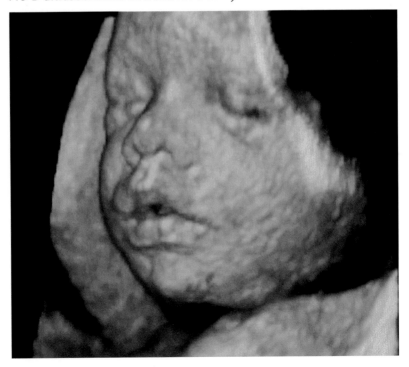

Genetic Testing

If a growth disorder is suspected based on an ultrasound, or if the family history alone causes concern, genetic testing may be recommended in order to confirm or rule out the diagnosis. These tests examine the DNA that makes up genes. Genetic testing can be done before or after birth. Growth disorders such as achondroplasia, Turner syndrome, Marfan syndrome, and osteogenesis imperfecta (brittle bone disease) can be diagnosed through genetic testing.

Diagnosing a genetic problem before birth or shortly after allows for early detection so that treatment can begin as early as possible. In 1991 the genes for Marfan syndrome were located on chromosomes 3 and 15, leading to the identification of the protein controlled by the gene. In 1994 researchers identified the gene that causes achondroplasia, located on chromosome 4. This discovery made it possible for expectant parents who both have achondroplasia to know whether or not their baby has inherited the fatal double dominant form of the condition.

Chorionic Villus Sampling

There are two ways that genetic testing can be done before birth. The first is called chorionic villus sampling. This procedure can be done fairly early in pregnancy, usually in about the tenth to the twelfth week. During this procedure, the doctor inserts a long, thin tube into the vagina, through the cervix, and into the uterus. This is known as transcervical chorionic villus sampling. The procedure can also be done by inserting a long needle through the abdominal wall and into the uterus. This is known as transabdominal chorionic villus sampling. Using ultrasound as a guide, a small tissue sample is taken from a part of the placenta called the chorionic villi. The tissue is sent to a lab, where the cells are examined for the specific genetic abnormality that causes the suspected disorder.

Amniocentesis

A second method of prenatal genetic testing is called amniocentesis. This procedure is done later in pregnancy, at about the fif-

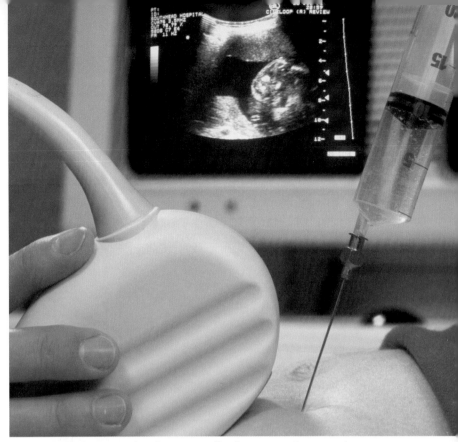

A doctor draws a sample of amniotic fluid using an ultrasound scan as a guide. The fetal cells can then be examined for genetic abnormalities.

teenth to the eighteenth week. Amniocentesis is similar to trans-abdominal chorionic villus sampling in that a long, very thin needle is inserted through the abdominal wall and into the uterus. Again using ultrasound as a guide, the doctor withdraws 1 to 2 tablespoons (15 to 30 ml) of amniotic fluid, which surrounds the baby. Living cells that have been shed by the baby into the fluid are allowed to grow in the lab for two to three weeks. They are then examined for genetic abnormalities.

Both chorionic villus sampling and amniocentesis take only a few minutes to perform. Most women feel little if any discomfort from either procedure. Both procedures carry a slight risk of causing a miscarriage. While results are not 100 percent guaranteed, both tests are highly accurate in diagnosing genetic abnormalities. When there is a risk of a genetic growth disorder, prenatal genetic testing allows parents to plan more fully for their baby's future.

Diagnosis After Birth

Some children with growth disorders can be diagnosed at the time of their birth, particularly those with skeletal dysplasias such as achondroplasia. That was the case for Cindy and Bob and their son Kevin, who was born with dwarfism. Both Cindy and Bob are of normal height, and there are no dwarfs in either family. Kevin was born a month premature, and he had respiratory problems. Bob remembers, "The doctor said, 'Your son is not normal and may never be normal.'" [12]

Skeletal dysplasias can often be diagnosed at birth. This X-ray shows a newborn with thanatophoric dysplasia.

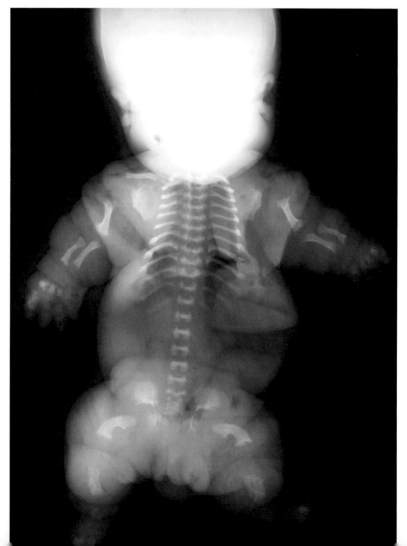

The diagnosis of a growth disorder often begins later, when a child's parents notice that the child seems to be the smallest or tallest one in his or her class, or that the child does not seem to be outgrowing his or her clothes. After second grade, Andrew, who had not always been short for his age, started to fall behind the other boys in his class. "He wore the same winter coat for three years,"[13] says his mother, Chris.

Growth Charts

One of the most important tools for early diagnosis of a growth disorder is an examination of the child's pattern of growth on a growth chart. By looking at where the child's height and weight fall on the chart over a period of months or years, the doctor can see whether or not growth is progressing normally. Even if a child's measurements are low on the chart, they should follow the curves on the chart fairly closely. Diagnosis of a problem with growth may begin when the child's doctor notices that the child's growth is not following the curves on the growth chart as it should. If they appear to be crossing the percentile lines, the doctor will want to find out if this is a normal variation of growth, such as constitutional growth delay or familial short stature, or if there is a more serious growth problem present. Growth problems are suspected when at least two percentile lines have been crossed.

At first, the doctor may simply want to watch the child's growth pattern over a year or two to see if it improves on its own. "To look at this pattern of growth, or a child's height velocity, you usually have to look at several years of growth," says one pediatrician. "Keep in mind that children may normally cross percentiles in the first few years of life, and this is actually a common finding in children with familial short stature or constitutional growth delay."[14]

History and Physical Examination

Another important early step in diagnosing a potential growth disorder in a child is a complete medical history. It is important for the doctor to determine if the child is actually growing

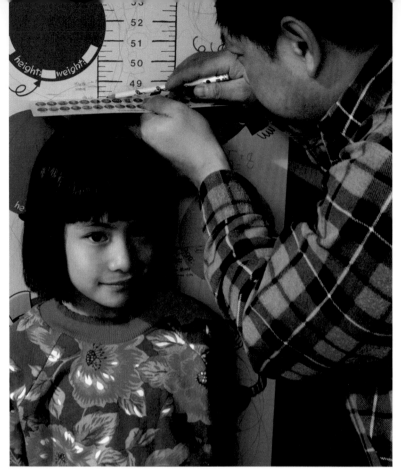

A little girl has her height measured on a growth chart.

abnormally or is simply short but growing normally for him or her. The doctor will ask about any medical problems that may have occurred during the mother's pregnancy or the early life of the child that could have affected his or her growth before and just after birth. The doctor will ask about the mother's diet during pregnancy and about any alcohol, tobacco, or drug use. He or she will want to know about the growth patterns of family members, especially the parents, including any genetic growth disorders in the family. In addition, the doctor will ask questions about the child's diet, appetite, and bowel patterns, checking for absorption problems. The doctor may also ask if there are any social problems at home or at school.

Along with the family history, the doctor will do a thorough physical examination of the child, looking for any physical signs or features associated with genetic disorders. For example, arms and legs that seem too short for the rest of the body may indicate a skeletal dysplasia. Excessively long arms, legs, fingers, and toes, a protruding breastbone, vision problems, and flat feet are signs of Marfan syndrome. At nearly 6 feet (1.82m) tall, signs of Marfan syndrome were already apparent in fifth-grader Nancy, who always knew she was different from her classmates. "I used to joke that I looked like I swallowed a cardboard box," she says. "Even though I was tall and thin, I had no waistline. I'd see other tall people, but they didn't look like me."[15]

The physical examination also checks for outward signs of problems with other organ systems that may affect the child's growth. For example, low urine output and dry, itchy skin may signal kidney disease, a common cause of growth failure. Obesity along with a slow growth rate are signs of Cushing's syndrome. Many symptoms occurring together, such as extremely short stature, easy fatigue, delayed teeth development in the young child, or delayed puberty in the older child, may indicate a deficiency of growth hormone or thyroid hormone.

A thorough physical examination will help a doctor determine if a child may have a growth disorder.

Bone Age X-Rays

If the physical exam and the growth charts indicate a possible growth problem, the doctor may order a bone age X-ray. Bone age is a way of describing the maturity of a person's bones and can be used to estimate final adult height. As a child grows, his or her bones change in size and shape until puberty, when they stop growing in response to hormonal signals. Bone age is the age at which children reach a particular stage of bone maturation. The X-ray is done on the child's fingers, hand, and wrist, where there are many bones. By comparing the appearance of the bones in the hand to a standard atlas of bone growth, the doctor can estimate how much more growth is possible. If there is a problem, such as growth hormone deficiency or hypothyroidism, the child's bone age will be delayed. An advanced bone age may indicate early onset of puberty, leading to the end of the child's growth.

In order to determine a child's rate of growth, an X-ray can be done of the child's hand. This is then compared to an X-ray of an adult's hand (below).

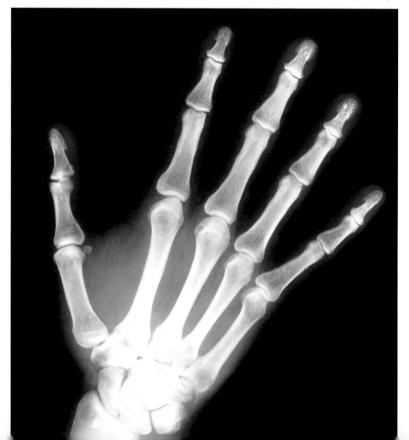

The Skeletal Survey

Another X-ray that is especially useful for confirming skeletal dysplasias is the skeletal survey. As its name suggests, this test involves taking X-rays of the entire skeleton to check for bone abnormalities that are associated with particular dysplasias. For example, in achondroplasia, the survey will show a large skull with a narrowed opening at the base (the foramen magnum); short, boxlike vertebrae; short, thick arm and leg bones with abnormally shaped growth plates; and shortened bones in the hands and fingers.

Liver Function Studies

A healthy liver is essential for proper growth because it is where insulin-like growth factor 1 (IGF-1) is produced in response to growth hormone. If it is not functioning properly, it will not produce IGF-1 in the necessary amounts for proper growth.

Several blood tests can be done to evaluate liver function. A serum albumin level measures the level of albumin, a protein that is synthesized by the liver. A low serum albumin can indicate liver disease, malnutrition, or a problem with absorption of nutrients. Abnormal amounts of chemicals called liver enzymes, which have important functions in metabolism, often indicate liver disease. An abnormally high level of bilirubin, a by-product of the breakdown of red blood cells, indicates liver disease because it is removed from the body by the liver.

Kidney Function Tests

Like the liver, the kidneys play a critical role in a child's growth, especially by regulating the body's ability to use vitamin D and the minerals calcium and phosphorus for bone growth. They may also have a role in the metabolism of growth hormone.

Tests that evaluate the kidneys include measurements of creatinine in the blood and in the urine and measurements of blood urea nitrogen. Creatinine is a metabolic waste product that is excreted into the urine by the kidneys. Too much creatinine in the blood and too little in the urine indicate that the kidneys are not filtering the blood as they should. Blood urea

The Pediatric Endocrinologist

When the medical history, physical examination, and early tests indicate a possible growth problem, a pediatric endocrinologist may be consulted. A pediatric endocrinologist is a doctor who specializes in the diagnosis and treatment of all endocrine problems in children and teens, including diabetes and other blood sugar problems, thyroid conditions, and pituitary tumors, as well as growth disorders. He or she must work closely with both the child and the parents and must also be skilled at working with children of all ages.

The pediatric endocrinologist will review all the information gathered by the pediatrician to make sure that nothing has been overlooked. He or she may order more specific lab tests to check the liver, kidneys, thyroid, adrenal glands, and the pituitary gland. He or she may also order genetic tests to look for other causes of the disorder. The pediatric endocrinologist will then decide on the best plan of treatment for the child and will work with the pediatrician to monitor the child's progress.

The specialty of pediatric endocrinology was pioneered by Dr. Lawson Wilkins at Johns Hopkins Medical School in Baltimore, Maryland, beginning in the late 1940s. Today, training for doctors in the specialty involves three years of extra training in pediatrics, followed by a two- to three-year fellowship, which provides specialized experience in pediatric endocrinology.

nitrogen is a by-product of protein metabolism that, like creatinine, is excreted by the kidneys. In kidney disease, the blood urea nitrogen is too high.

Endocrine Tests

If there are no problems with other organ systems that explain a growth problem, the pediatric endocrinologist may perform studies to evaluate the function of other endocrine systems. The thyroid gland, located at the base of the throat, has an important role in growth because it produces thyroid hormones, commonly called T4 and T3, which regulate metabolism and bone growth. A simple blood test can measure the levels of thyroid hormones in the blood. Thyroid-stimulating hormone from the pituitary is also measured to make sure that the problem is not actually in the pituitary.

Sometimes, problems with the thyroid can lead to problems with the adrenal glands as well. The adrenal glands, located at the top of each kidney, affect growth by producing cortisol, which regulates the metabolism of sugar, protein, fats, and carbohydrates. Too much cortisol, a condition known as Cushing's syndrome, can cause growth retardation in children. Adrenal function is tested by measuring the blood levels of cortisol and ACTH, the hormone from the pituitary that stimulates the adrenals.

Testing the Pituitary Gland

Problems with the thyroid or the adrenals do not always start in the gland itself; they may be symptoms of a problem with the pituitary in its role as the master gland. For this reason, the endocrinologist will want to test the function of the pituitary as well, to make sure it is sending the right signals to the other glands by producing thyroid-stimulating hormone and ACTH in the right amounts. The endocrinologist will also perform tests that show whether the pituitary is making enough growth hormone. If the level of one or more of these hormones is too low, a condition called hypopituitarism or pituitary insufficiency may exist. Simple blood tests can measure these hormones.

Measuring Growth Hormone

Measuring growth hormone is somewhat more complicated than measuring thyroid-stimulating hormone or ACTH. This is because growth hormone is produced in irregular spurts throughout the day and night, with about two-thirds of it being made during sleep. Also, growth hormone does not stay in the bloodstream very long before it is used by the cells. For these reasons, testing just one blood sample does not give an accurate

Charting Growth

Beginning in the 1960s, a survey called the National Health and Nutrition Examination Survey (NHANES) was taken of height and weight measurements of thousands of American children. In 1977 the data gathered from the survey was put together and used to develop a special graph called a standard growth chart. Curved lines on the chart, called percentiles, show where a child's height and weight ought to be for each sex and for all ages up to twenty years. There are special charts for babies who are born prematurely and for children born with certain health conditions that affect growth.

When a child is weighed and measured by a doctor, the measurements are plotted on a growth chart and compared to the standard for other children of the same age and sex. If a child's height measurement lands near the 75th percentile line, for example, it means that the child is taller than 75 percent of children his or her age and sex and shorter than 25 percent. However, as one pediatrician explains:

When evaluating children who are short, more important than where they are on the growth chart is how they have been growing. Children who are growing normally should follow their growth curve fairly closely, so even if they are at the 5th or 3rd percentile, if that is where they have always been, then they are probably growing normally. If a child is crossing percentiles, or lines on the growth curve, then there may be a medical problem causing him to be short.

Some doctors feel that any child who grows less than 2 inches (5cm) per year after his or her second birthday should be examined more closely for a growth problem.

"Question of the Week - Short Children," by Dr. Vincent Ianelli, 2006. http://pediatrics. about.com/cs/weeklyquestion/a/04032_ask.htm.

picture of how the pituitary is working. Several samples, drawn over a period of time, are needed. Endocrinologist JonBen Svoboda explains the difficulties in diagnosing acromegaly, the overproduction of growth hormone after puberty:

If we just measure a growth hormone level, patients with acromegaly can have a normal level, and normal people can have a growth hormone level five times above normal. This is because growth hormone secretion is always changing. A much more stable screening test is IGF-1, which is a protein made by the liver in response to secretion of growth hormone from the pituitary. If growth hormone levels are consistently high over time, the IGF-1 level will likely be elevated. [16]

The Growth Hormone Stimulation Test

A growth hormone stimulation test (also called an arginine test) is a laboratory study that specifically evaluates the production of growth hormone by the pituitary gland when a deficiency is suspected. To do this test, a small, plastic catheter (an IV) is inserted into a vein in the arm or hand. A sample of blood is drawn as a baseline measurement. Then an amino acid called arginine, which is known to stimulate the release of growth hormone from the pituitary, is given through the IV over a period of thirty minutes. Sometimes growth hormone–releasing hormone, made by the hypothalamus, is used instead of or in addition to the arginine. Four more blood samples are then drawn out through the IV at thirty-minute intervals, and the level of growth hormone in each sample is measured. If the levels are low, it indicates that the pituitary is not responding properly. Often, the samples are also tested for IGF-1, which, unlike growth hormone, remains at a more constant level throughout the day and is therefore easier to measure.

Growth Hormone Suppression Test

Gigantism and acromegaly involve the opposite problem— too much growth hormone rather than too little. The growth hormone suppression test is done when one of these disorders is suspected. For this test, an IV is inserted into a vein and a baseline sample is drawn. The patient is then asked to drink a solution of water containing about 2.5 to 3.5 ounces

(75 to 100 g) of glucose, or sugar. The solution is very sweet, but it has to be finished within five minutes or the results may not be accurate. Two more blood samples are drawn one to two hours after the glucose solution is finished. Glucose and growth hormone levels are measured in each sample. A high level of glucose in the blood signals the hypothalamus to shut off growth hormone production by the pituitary. If the pituitary is functioning properly, the growth hormone level should drop in response to the glucose. If it does not, it means that the pituitary is not responding to the instructions from the hypothalamus.

Diagnosing Pituitary Tumors

If laboratory tests indicate that there is in fact a problem in the pituitary, the next step is to find out what is causing the problem so it can be treated. If there is no history of any illness or injury involving the brain to explain the problem, a tumor in the pituitary or hypothalamus may be the cause.

There are two major kinds of tumors that can affect growth in this way. The first is called a craniopharyngioma. This is a benign tumor that grows in the area of the hypothalamus and the pituitary. As it grows, it creates pressure inside the head and can press on these structures, interfering with their function. It can also press on the optic nerves, causing vision problems. Hormone imbalances, severe headaches, and visual disturbances are symptoms of a craniopharyngioma.

The second kind of tumor is called a pituitary adenoma. This is also a benign tumor that grows in the pituitary itself. Pituitary adenomas may secrete one or more pituitary hormones, but they do not respond to signals from the hypothalamus. If the adenoma secretes thyroid-stimulating hormone, the thyroid will become overactive. If it secretes ACTH, then the adrenals will make too much cortisol, and Cushing's syndrome results. An adenoma that secretes growth hormone can cause pituitary gigantism in children and acromegaly in adults.

The diagnosis of both of these tumors starts with looking at the hormonal and physical symptoms that they cause. Diagno-

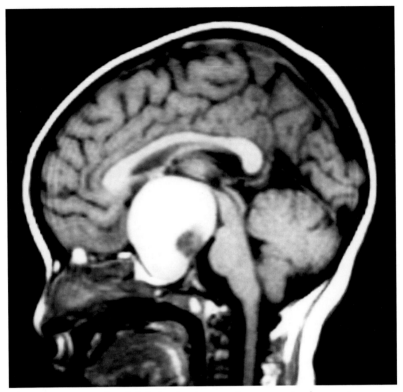

This MRI image of a child's brain shows a large craniopharyngioma, which is a benign tumor.

sis is confirmed using sophisticated imaging procedures such as computerized axial tomography (CT scan) and magnetic resonance imaging (MRI). A CT scan uses special X-ray equipment to get images of the brain from several different angles. The views are joined together by a computer to show a cross section of the brain and the structures inside it. The CT scan can provide more detailed information about the brain than regular X-rays because it can show the anatomy of soft tissues, such as brain tissue and blood vessels, as well as the harder bone. A tumor shows on the CT scan as a roughly circular white area that would not be present on a normal scan.

An MRI does not use X-rays at all. It uses radio waves and a strong magnetic field to create clear and detailed images of structures inside the body. Dina recalls her son Cameron's experience

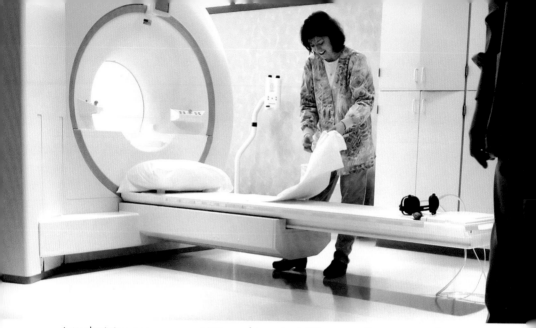

A technician prepares an MRI machine. An MRI uses radio waves and a strong magnetic field to create detailed images of the body.

with MRIs: "They did an MRI (shortly after he was born) to make sure he did not have hydrocephalus, and to make sure his spinal cord wasn't getting pinched in his neck. We would go every six months, then the doctor bumped it to every year, and then when we saw him at the age of four, he said every other year."[17] Newer MRI technology can even demonstrate brain function as well as its structure.

CHAPTER THREE

Treating Growth Disorders

For most growth disorders, there is no real cure. The goal of treatment is to prevent and manage the physical symptoms the disorder may cause, as well as any social and emotional issues the individual and his or her family must deal with. For some, treatment may be simply a matter of replacing a deficient hormone. For others, surgery may be necessary. For all growth disorders, however, the goals of treatment are to maximize the quality of life for the individual and to help him or her accept and live with his or her final adult height.

Treatment of Organ System Problems

If a problem with growth is related to a particular organ system, treatment is aimed at correcting that system. Diseases of the liver and kidneys have an especially significant effect on a child's growth, especially if they are present at birth or in infancy.

Liver diseases can cause growth retardation because they interfere with the liver's ability to carry out its many important functions, including the production of the growth hormone IGF-1 and the storage and metabolism of nutrients. Most liver diseases in young children are difficult to treat because they can cause severe damage to the tiny tubes, or ducts, that carry bile out of the liver. Special diets and medications can help to alleviate some of the symptoms of diseases such as biliary atresia and neonatal hepatitis, both of which cause severe damage to the

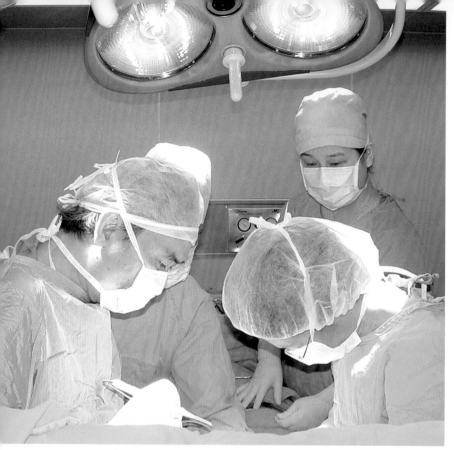

A group of surgeons performs a liver transplant.

liver. When the damage becomes so advanced that the child's life is in danger, the only treatment is liver transplant surgery.

Most transplanted livers come from donors who have recently died. An entire liver or just part of one may be transplanted. Living family members may be able to donate part of their own liver if their tissues are a close match to the child's. A child who receives a liver transplant must take medications for the rest of his or her life that help prevent the body's immune system from rejecting the new liver.

Several factors affect the success of the liver transplant, such as the age of the child, the extent of the liver damage, the quality of the tissue match, the medical and surgical techniques used, and proper care after surgery. Survival rates reach 90 to 95 percent after the first year. Most children have increased growth rates after a liver transplant, and most parents rate their child's quality of life as good or very good.

Kidney Disease

Healthy kidneys are also necessary for normal growth. Diseased kidneys cannot perform their functions of filtering waste products and extra fluid from the blood, activating vitamin D, and balancing calcium and phosphorus. Children in renal failure also may not respond normally to growth hormone. They often have little appetite and do not eat enough. Also, some medications used to treat illnesses that cause renal failure can stunt growth.

Good nutrition is especially important for growth in children with renal failure. Foods high in phosphorus must be restricted because too much phosphorus prevents calcium from getting into the bones. These foods include dairy products, meat, fish, poultry, broccoli, peas, and dark breads. Doctors work closely with dieticians to find ways to lower dietary phosphorus and still maintain a healthy intake of vitamins, minerals, and protein. Medications

An MRI of a twenty-two-year-old woman with scoliosis, which is a lateral curvature of the upper spine.

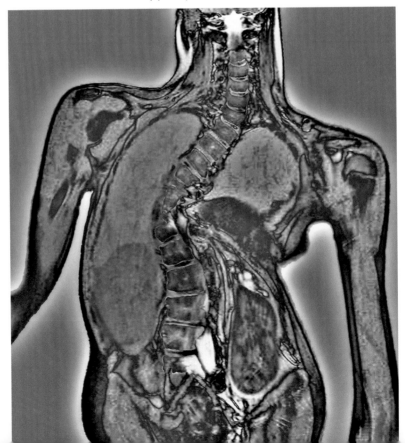

called phosphate binders, which prevent phosphorus from getting into the bloodstream, may also be used. The child may also take extra calcium and the vitamin D hormone calcitriol.

A major goal of treating kidney disease is to keep the child as healthy as possible until a kidney transplant can be done. About half of all transplanted kidneys come from living donors—a close family member or family friend who is a good match. As with liver transplants, the child must take antirejection medication for the rest of his or her life.

Treating Endocrine Disorders

As with disorders of other organ systems, the treatment of poor growth caused by endocrine disorders depends on the particular gland involved. The thyroid gland, the adrenal glands, and especially the pituitary gland have important roles in normal growth.

Thyroid hormone, produced by the thyroid gland, acts like the gas pedal in a car. It stimulates the cells to increase their metabolism, leading to cell growth. If there is not enough thyroid hormone, the cells slow down, like a car does when the brake is put on, and growth slows. This is one of the signs of the condition called hypothyroidism. Hypothyroidism can be present at birth, or it may show up later in childhood or adolescence. If left untreated in a newborn, it can lead to a severe form of mental retardation and other developmental problems. Hypothyroidism is relatively easy to treat by replacing the deficient hormone in tablet form and then closely watching thyroid levels over time. Depending on the cause of the deficiency, the child may need to take thyroid hormone for the rest of his or her life. Some children seem eventually to outgrow the disorder. Once treatment is started, most children experience catch-up growth.

Cushing's Syndrome

Problems with the thyroid gland can cause malfunction of the adrenal glands as well. Cushing's syndrome is a disorder of the adrenal glands in which too much of the hormone cortisol is produced. It can be caused by a pituitary adenoma, adrenal tumors, or other cancerous tumors that secrete ACTH, which stimulates

To Treat or Not to Treat—Growth Hormone Therapy for Healthy Kids

In 2003 the FDA approved the use of growth hormone for children who are very short but have no apparent medical cause for their short stature. This decision was controversial. Many physicians had already been prescribing growth hormone for their shortest patients since the 1980s, without FDA approval, a practice called off-label use.

Supporters of the decision say that healthy short adults face the same obstacles in life as do those who are short for medical reasons, and that it is unfair to deny treatment to children who are willing to take the daily injections and whose parents are willing to pay the cost of twenty-five thousand to thirty thousand dollars per year. Debra Counts, an endocrinologist at the University of Maryland, says, "I've had kids come into the clinic and tell me they were ridiculed—locked inside a locker at school or stuffed into a trash can because they were small. Yes, short stature is not an organic disease, but it is a problem that causes a diminished quality of life."

Critics of the decision say that the drug companies are profiting from a condition that is more of a cosmetic concern than a medical problem. "Society is buying into the idea that someone who's short has a medical problem," says Nancy Worcester, a professor at the University of Wisconsin—Madison.

Growth hormone treatment also carries certain rare but possibly serious side effects, such as increased pressure on the brain, joint problems, and diabetes. Response to growth hormone treatment is unpredictable, and questions remain as to whether or not the risks and costs outweigh the possible benefits.

Debra Counts, "Drugs Can Make Short Kids Grow But Is It Right to Prescribe Them?," *People*, 9/15/2003. Vol. 60, Iss. 11, pp. 103-104.

Nancy Worcester, "My How You've Grown," *Business Week*, 11/28/2005, Iss. 3961, pp. 86-88.

the adrenals to secrete cortisol. Too much cortisol in children, though rare, can cause slowed growth rates. Treatment of Cushing's syndrome depends on the cause of the disease and may include surgery to remove ACTH-secreting tumors, followed by radiation therapy and chemotherapy. Drugs may be given that inhibit the production of cortisol.

Treating Pituitary Disorders

Disorders of the pituitary gland are a frequent cause of problems in the other endocrine glands. If the pituitary produces inappropriate amounts of its trophic hormones, such as thyroid-stimulating hormone and ACTH, then their target glands cannot do their jobs properly. If the pituitary fails to produce enough growth hormone, growth failure results. If it produces too much, the child will be abnormally tall.

As with the other endocrine disorders, treatment of pituitary disorders depends on the cause of the disorder. If the diagnosis shows that the pituitary is not producing enough growth hormone—a condition called growth hormone deficiency—the deficiency is treated with injections of a synthetic form of growth hormone, produced using recombinant, or artificially made, DNA technology. Some children must receive injections every day; others may only need them three or four times a week. An improvement in growth rate is usually noticed after three to four months. Growth hormone injections can increase final adult height if they are started early enough. As one growth expert explains, "It is widely believed that treatment should begin early for a child to reach his or her full growth potential, and there are some data to support initiating treatment before age five."[18]

Treatment with growth hormone usually lasts several years, until the child reaches an acceptable height or has reached his or her maximum growth potential. There is a great deal of variation in how kids respond to growth hormone treatment. Some gain very little height, while others shoot up as much as 10 to 12 inches (25 to 30 cm). In the fourth grade, Angelo was so short he was often mistaken for a kindergartner. "I was picked on a lot," he says. "Other kids called me 'midget' and 'shrimp.' I used to cry." [19] His mother persuaded his doctor to prescribe injections of growth hormone. Now nineteen, Angelo stands at 5 feet 9 inches (1.75m), a full 10 inches (25cm) taller than doctors predicted his adult height would be.

In 1998 Serono Laboratories introduced a new treatment for growth hormone deficiency caused by the failure of growth hormone–releasing hormone, made in the hypothalamus of the brain, to trigger the release of growth hormone from the pituitary. The new drug triggers the release of available growth hormone so that it can be used by the body. The same company also created a new test that doctors can use that helps them tell whether the dysfunction is in the pituitary or in the hypothalamus.

A deficiency in growth hormone often leads to a deficiency in the other important growth hormone, IGF-1, which is made in response to growth hormone. In addition, about six thousand children a year who have short stature are diagnosed with primary IGF-1 deficiency (IGFD). This means that their growth hormone levels are normal, but they are still not making enough IGF-1. In 2005 the FDA approved two new drugs for the treatment of IGFD, both of which contain synthetic, or man-made, forms of IGF-1 and are identical to naturally produced IGF-1. Studies are ongoing that will determine the long-term effectiveness of this relatively new treatment for short stature.

Surgical Treatment for Pituitary Disorders

If the diagnostic process has shown that the cause of the malfunctioning pituitary is a tumor, then surgery to remove the tumor is often performed. As long as the tumor has not invaded surrounding tissue and the patient is healthy enough to tolerate the stress of surgery, this is usually the first choice of treatment for pituitary tumors.

The two major types of tumors that cause pituitary problems are craniopharyngioma and pituitary adenoma. Adenomas that secrete pituitary hormones are called functioning

Preventing Organ Transplant Rejection

In many cases the only way to stop the progression of a chronic liver or kidney disease is with an organ transplant. A major obstacle to overcome after the surgery is organ rejection, in which the recipient's immune system recognizes the new organ as foreign tissue and attacks it. If this happens, the new organ will fail. Several measures help to prevent this from happening.

Tissue matching, done before transplant surgery, involves several tests to make sure that the donor organ will be a close match to the recipient's tissues. ABO blood typing checks the blood type of both donor and recipient to make sure that they are the same or at least compatible with each other. Human leukocyte antigen typing is another test that looks for antigens, or genetic markers on white blood cells, which play an important role in the immune system. Their identification helps determine the compatibility of donor tissue with the recipient. A cross match makes sure that the recipient's blood does not contain antibodies to the donor's tissue. Serology tests make sure that the donor does not have any diseases such as hepatitis or HIV that can be transmitted to the recipient.

After the transplant, the recipient must take antirejection drugs for the rest of his or her life. These drugs, called immunosuppressants, suppress the immune system to prevent or reverse rejection. There are many side effects, however, and suppressing the immune system also means that the recipient will be less able to fight off infections. The good news is that, with close monitoring, frequent checkups, and following the doctor's instructions, the great majority of organ transplant recipients can work, travel, play sports, go to school, and enjoy healthy and active lives.

tumors. They may secrete ACTH, thyroid-stimulating hormone, or growth hormone, as well as other pituitary hormones. Pituitary adenomas are the most common cause of gigantism in children and acromegaly in adults. Neither of these tumors is malignant, but they can grow and create other problems, such as headaches and visual disturbances.

Surgery for these tumors is usually done through a transphenoidal approach, meaning the tumor can be reached by going through the sphenoid sinus, a hollow, air-filled cavity behind the nose. With the aid of a powerful operating microscope, the surgeon uses delicate instruments to remove as much of the soft tumor tissue as possible. Some surgeons, instead of using a microscope, use a long, slender telescope called an endoscope to look at the tumor through the opening in the back of the sinus. The eyepiece of the endoscope is attached to a special camera, which is then connected to a video monitor similar to a television screen.

If the tumor has grown beyond the area that can be seen by the surgeon, he or she may not be able to remove all of it. Sometimes a second surgery may be necessary to remove larger tumors. The most common risk is damage to the normal part of the pituitary, meaning that hormone replacement may still be necessary after the surgery.

Radiation Therapy

If there is remaining tumor tissue after surgery, it can be treated with radiation therapy to stop it from growing further. It is also done for patients who are not healthy enough to undergo surgery and for patients who do not improve after surgery and medication. For some patients, radiation treatments may be done before or even instead of surgery. Radiation therapy uses high-energy penetrating waves of radioactive particles such as X-rays, gamma rays, proton beams, or neutron rays to destroy or stop the growth of tumor cells. It works by damaging the DNA of the cells so they cannot divide further.

There are two ways of delivering the radiation. In external radiation therapy, the beam of radiation is directed from outside the body at the area of the tumor. In internal radiation, the radioactive material is implanted into the body near the tumor. When the implant has been in for the prescribed length of time, it is removed. Radiation therapy is painless and usually does not require the patient to stay in the hospital overnight.

Drug Treatment for Acromegaly

In addition to transphenoidal surgery to remove pituitary tumors, there are medications that can be used to treat acromegaly. Medications can be used to shrink tumors before surgery or as follow-up treatment after surgery. The two major types of drugs are called somatostatin analogs and dopamine agonists. These medications work in two ways. One is by lowering growth hormone levels, which will improve the physical signs of acromegaly. The other is by preventing pituitary tumors from becoming larger or by actually decreasing the tumor size.

A new group of medications for acromegaly are called growth hormone receptor antagonists. Antagonist medications work by blocking the effects of growth hormone on the body's cells. They also help to improve the symptoms of acromegaly.

Treating Skeletal Dysplasias

Unlike endocrine growth disorders or growth retardation caused by other organ system failures, disorders that are genetic in nature cannot be treated directly. The goals of treatment for disorders such as achondroplasia and Marfan syndrome are to alleviate the symptoms and physical challenges presented by the disorder.

Skeletal dysplasias, of which there are more than two hundred types, present a wide variety of symptoms that affect several body systems. Each individual will have his or her own set of physical challenges that must be dealt with. Many of these can be effectively treated.

The growth and development of children with skeletal dysplasias such as achondroplasia must be watched closely. Special growth charts are used that have been specifically designed for children with achondroplasia. Skeletal abnormalities are also monitored closely so that potential complications can be treated early. For example, if the head is getting too large, the child will be tested for hydrocephalus, a condition in which too much fluid builds up inside the skull, causing pressure on the brain. If this happens, a neurosurgeon will insert a special drain called a shunt into the brain that drains the excess fluid out of the head and into the abdominal cavity, where it is reabsorbed by the body. Hilary's daughter, Kate, developed hydrocephalus after being treated for an abscess in her brain. "For six weeks her hydrocephalus was untreated and her head circumference grew daily," says Hilary. "A CT scan after five weeks showed the abscesses were gone. Two weeks later Kate received her shunt. Her head went down quite a bit and she continues to catch up to it as she grows." [20]

Compression of the upper end of the spinal cord is another complication that happens when the opening in the bottom of the skull, called the foramen magnum, is too small. This can cause serious problems with breathing, such as snoring and sleep apnea, in which the child actually stops breathing during sleep. In very young children, sudden death can result. Surgery can widen the opening and relieve pressure on the spinal cord, but the procedure can be dangerous, too. Explains one surgeon, "You're working in a very tight spot with extremely sensitive structures." [21] In cases of severe airway obstruction when these methods cannot help, a tracheotomy may be needed. A tracheotomy is a small opening in the trachea, or windpipe, at the base of the throat, through which the child can breathe.

The spinal cord can also become compressed if the canal in the backbone through which the cord passes is too narrow, a condition called spinal stenosis. Spinal stenosis can cause pain, numbness, and tingling in the arms or legs. An operation called a laminectomy widens the canal and relieves the pressure.

Small facial structures can cause several problems. A small jaw may cause the teeth to be overcrowded, requiring extra dental care and sometimes braces. In addition, the tonsils can obstruct the upper airway and contribute to breathing problems. Removing the tonsils and adenoids (lymph tissue near the tonsils) can help. Children with achondroplasia also get frequent ear infections. This can lead to hearing loss. Tiny ear tubes can be inserted into the eardrum to relieve the pressure caused by the infections and prevent hearing loss.

Kyphosis is a spinal abnormality that causes an abnormal curvature of the upper spine. It usually occurs because the baby's back muscles are too weak to support normal posture. It often goes away after the child begins to walk, but if it does not, a back brace may be needed to correct it. If the brace does not work, the child may need to wear a cast on his or her torso for several months. In extreme cases, surgery may be necessary to return the spine to its normal curve.

When a child with achondroplasia begins to walk, other orthopedic problems may arise because vertical posture causes weight-bearing pressures on the lower body. Lordosis is an overcurvature of the lower spine that can cause back and leg pain and problems with walking. The extra pressure can also cause the leg bones to bow outward, also causing problems with gait. Some people with very bowed legs choose to have orthopedic surgery to straighten the legs. Others choose to live with their body the way it is. Sue had this decision to make when she was younger. She explains:

> My legs are very bowed and I've never had them corrected. My mother was concerned, she always took me for annual check-ups at the Crippled Children's Hospital, and they considered surgery but they really didn't know how to do it. They talked about breaking my legs and resetting them, which we know today is the wrong thing to do. Even so, I was pretty active, I rode a bike, went roller skating. [22]

Children with achondroplasia also tend to gain too much weight, which can worsen skeletal problems such as lordosis and bowed legs. Proper diet and nutritional guidance for the child and his or her family help to prevent obesity.

Controversial Treatments

Some treatments for skeletal dysplasias are controversial. At some medical centers, doctors are studying the effectiveness of giving injections of human growth hormone to children with achondroplasia. So far, some children have experienced some increase in growth over one to two years, but it is not yet known whether this treatment will significantly improve their adult height. The treatment is expensive, however, and the injections are uncomfortable. Many people feel that, since achondroplasia is not caused by a deficiency of growth hormone, this is not an appropriate treatment. They feel that it is better for children with achondroplasia to learn to accept themselves as they are, rather than endure this lengthy and expensive therapy.

Limb-Lengthening Surgery

Another controversial treatment is limb-lengthening surgery. In this operation, the long bones of the legs are cut and a bone lengthening device is put on the legs. Over a period of several months, the device gradually separates the ends of the bones. As new bone tissue forms between the cut ends, the length of the bones is increased. This treatment can add as much as 12 inches (30cm) to a person's height, but it is controversial because it takes a long time and is expensive. It is also extremely painful. Some pain medications actually slow bone growth. Others are highly addictive. Pain can interfere with the physical therapy that is necessary and can prevent the patient from getting enough sleep. There is also the risk of complications such as bone infection, injury to nerves and blood vessels, failure

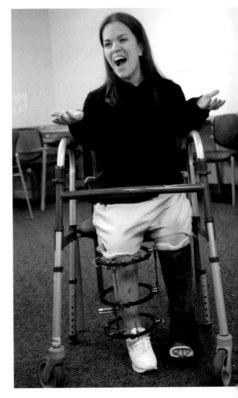

A woman who has undergone limb-lengthening surgery smiles as she demonstrates that she can now touch the floor while sitting in a chair.

of new bone growth, unequal limb lengths, and misshapen legs. Because this operation only adds height and does not treat any medical condition, many physicians and members of the dwarf community feel that it should not be done without careful consideration on the part of the individual and his or her family.

Treatment for Marfan Syndrome

As with other genetic disorders of growth, there is no cure for Marfan syndrome. The goal of treatment is to manage whatever symptoms the person has. Orthopedic braces or surgery may be necessary to correct skeletal deformities. Glasses or contact lenses can help with visual disturbances. Medications can ease pain associated with nervous system involvement. It is especially important for people with Marfan syndrome to avoid smoking, because they are already at risk for lung problems.

Sometimes leaking heart valves can be treated with medications that strengthen the heart and its valves. Other cases may require surgery to replace the valves. The most dangerous complication of Marfan syndrome involves a weakened aorta, the largest artery in the body. Ultrasound or CT scans may be used to watch the aorta over time. If it starts to expand, surgery is done to replace the weakened part with a stronger, artificial material. If it tears, it is a life-threatening emergency for which immediate surgery is the only treatment. Medications used to treat high blood pressure are helpful in preventing this complication.

Hope for a Better Life

While the great majority of growth disorders cannot be cured, it is clear that there are a tremendous number of options for treating them and their related symptoms. Scientists and physicians are constantly searching for and discovering new ways to treat these disorders and improve the quality of life for those affected. Ongoing research in the fields of genetics and genetic engineering, hormone replacement, medical and surgical intervention, and pharmacology is providing people with growth disorders a great deal of optimism for a happy and fulfilling life.

CHAPTER FOUR

Living with Growth Disorders

People with growth disorders face many different challenges. It can be difficult to adapt to a society that seems to be designed for those of average height. Besides the physical difficulties of just being very short or very tall, most growth disorders also involve health issues that must be dealt with. Even for those without other health problems, social and economic concerns are always present for those living with a growth disorder.

Getting Within Reach

Extreme shortness can interfere with normal activities of daily living that people of average height take for granted. Simple activities like driving a car, turning on lights, and grocery shopping can pose significant obstacles for those who are very short. Short arms and legs can make things like climbing stairs and carrying shopping bags very difficult. Cameron's mother, Dina, says, "He can't open the car door to get into the car. And he can't latch the seat belt because his arms are too short."[23] At school, Cameron says that buying his lunch is difficult. "Especially the wide trays! I normally have to carry it sideways. Luckily, I got muscles!"[24] Fortunately, there are dozens of products available that help people of short stature adapt to their world.

Peter Ojtozy demonstrates one of the problems people with dwarfism face, that of reaching a pay phone built for a person of average size.

Adaptive Driving Equipment

For people of short stature, driving presents challenges in terms of both reach and safety. Adaptive products are available that allow very short people to drive safely and comfortably.

Pedal extensions are available that allow the short person to reach the gas and brake pedals while still maintaining a natural, comfortable position on the seat. Some pedal extensions also include a false floor that allows the person to rest the foot not being used to drive the vehicle, so that it does not dangle uncomfortably. Pedal extensions also allow the driver to switch quickly from one pedal to the other if necessary.

Special seat cushions can be added that raise the driver up and allow him to see clearly through the windshield and into the rearview mirrors. They also provide extra support for the back and legs. Sitting at the proper height on the seat also allows the seat belt to fit properly across the body.

Automobile airbags can be hazardous to the short person who is not positioned properly on the seat. Airbags have been designed, according to government regulations, for people of average height. A short adult with short arms can be seriously injured if they are too low or too close to the airbag when it deploys. Along with a seat cushion for added height, steering column extensions can be inserted that bring the steering wheel closer to the driver so that he or she can be the recommended 10 to 12 inches (25 to 30 cm) away from the airbag.

Adaptive Items for Daily Living

Many different kinds of adaptations must be made around the home for people of short stature. In the kitchen, specially designed utensils such as vegetable peelers, jar and can openers,

There are many specially designed kitchen products to help people with short arms and fingers.

stove knob turners, button pushers, and eating utensils help those with short arms and fingers. Step stools are helpful for reaching sinks, stove tops, and countertops. Many dwarf families have counters that are custom-made at a lower level so that stools are not needed.

Light switch extensions attach to the switch and allow the person to turn lights on and off. There are also voice-activated light switches that turn the light on or off in response to a person's voice command. Doorknob attachments make it easier for people with very small hands to turn doorknobs. Special canes with platforms at the end make it easier to go up and down stairs by decreasing the height of the steps. There are special carts on low wheels for carrying shopping bags, groceries, books, and other items. Combination washer/dryers with one front-loading door make doing laundry easier by doing both washing and drying in one machine so that laundry does not have to be loaded and unloaded from large, top-loading machines.

Several companies make furniture specifically designed for short people. Chairs and couches have lower seats. Ergonomic work chairs have adjustable backs, seats, arms, and foot rests. Desks and work tables have shorter legs. Padded booster seats add height and extra back and neck support for children with weak muscles.

Finding clothing that is fashionable, age-appropriate, and well-fitting can be difficult for little people. Clothing is available that is specifically designed for their needs. Shirts and pants have shorter sleeves and legs. Shoes are designed for shorter, wider feet. T-shirts for kids are made that celebrate their special differences with slogans on them such as "Dwarf Princess" and "Little Things Mean a Lot."

Many other products exist that help a person of short stature adapt to an average-sized world. There are special bicycles for short children, with a low center of gravity, wide tires, high seat backs, and special hand grips. There are kits for travelers that include closet-bar adapters, step stools, and reaching and grabbing devices. Specialized products exist to help the short-statured person in almost every facet of his or her life.

Willem, a boy with achondroplasia, describes how he has adapted to life as a little person:

I'm not going to pretend that my height isn't a challenge. It is. Light switches and counters are usually too high for me. I can't reach some shelves in the grocery stores. It takes me three steps to keep up with one step of an average-size adult. And my mom has to hem almost all of my pants. But everyone faces challenges. You just have to face them with a good attitude. So I have a long barbeque fork to pull things down from pantry shelves. I'm a great climber, and I can make a stool out of just about anything. I'll even be able to drive a car, with the help of pedal extensions. If all else fails, I ask for help. The way I see it, I can do just about anything that an average-size person can do.[25]

Health Challenges

Besides having to adapt to the challenges of everyday living, people with growth disorders, especially skeletal dysplasias such as achondroplasia, often must live with health problems that are associated with their condition. Medical procedures and surgeries are part of the lives of most dwarfs. Dina explains: "We've had a lot of doctors. The ENT [ear, nose, and throat specialist] we would see regularly. Cameron's on his fourth set of ear tubes. They did an MRI to make sure he didn't have hydrocephalus, and to make sure his spinal cord wasn't getting pinched. We would go every six months, then the doctor bumped it to every year, and then when we saw him at age four, he said every other year."[26] In his six years, Cameron has also had his club foot fixed, his heel tendon lengthened, two hernia surgeries, and surgery to straighten his left leg.

Breathing problems are common for people with skeletal abnormalities. Because of smaller throat and facial structures and sometimes muscle weakness due to an impaired nervous system, their upper airway can become obstructed by the tongue, the tonsils, or other throat tissue, especially during sleep. This can cause

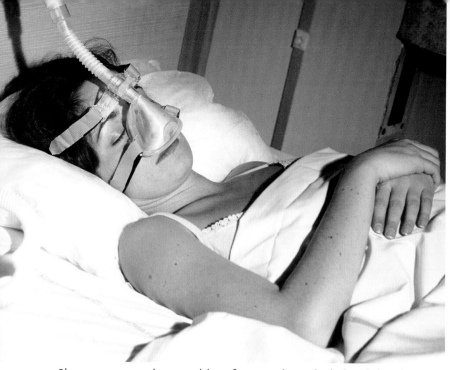

Sleep apnea can be a problem for people with skeletal dysplasias. Here a woman undergoes continuous positive airway pressure treatment for her sleep apnea.

sleep apnea—periods of time lasting several seconds when the person completely stops breathing during sleep. Surgery may help alleviate this problem, but sometimes other measures are necessary. One method of treating sleep apnea is known as continuous positive airway pressure. A small mask is worn over the nose or the nose and mouth and secured to the head with straps. A machine connected to the mask blows slightly pressurized air through the mask and into the airway, keeping it open during sleep and preventing sleep apnea. "Over the last few years," says one researcher, "we have been very successful with the use of nasal mask ventilation in children with sleep apnea, including those with achondroplasia. This [reduces] the need for tracheotomy, and results in a vast improvement in the quality of life for these patients."[27]

If a person has to have a tracheotomy in order to breathe, special measures are necessary to take care of it. The stoma, the opening at the base of the throat through which the person breathes, must be cleansed every day and kept free of the normal secretions that are made in the trachea, or it may get blocked. Sometimes the trachea will need to be suctioned free of these secretions, as the stoma prevents normal coughing. The plastic tube that goes inside the stoma must also be cleaned regularly. After several months, the trachea will decrease the amount of secretions it makes, so care of the stoma is easier.

Limited Mobility

It is estimated that 70 percent of all achondroplastic people live with frequent pain in their backs and legs because of spinal problems. About half of achondroplastic children under age ten have trouble with compression of the spine, causing pain and limping. One specialist explains: "They may walk for several blocks before they develop numbness, tingling, heavy sensations, weakness, tiredness. . . . Rather than admit symptoms for social reasons, the little person may stop to window shop frequently, or he may stop, stoop and tie his shoelace repeatedly."[28] Lightweight scooters are available to help a person who has difficulty walking long distances. Bowed legs and abnormal curvature of the spine can also cause difficulty getting around.

The Role of Orthopedics

Orthopedics is another specialty that plays a large role in the lives of people with skeletal dysplasias. Most patients will have some type of orthopedic procedure during their lives. For children who are still growing and develop kyphosis of the upper spine, a kyphosis brace may be recommended. There are several different kinds of kyphosis braces. They are worn on the upper part of the torso and neck, and gradually help the upper spine regain a more normal curve. Children who wear a kyphosis brace can still participate in most activities despite the brace, but it takes a while to get used to wearing it. Braces must be used carefully, and not every patient will benefit. One doctor explains, "Braces can be helpful. The problem comes in knowing when to brace. Many young children with this disorder have kyphosis early on but then outgrow it. Unnecessary braces can present problems of their own."[29] Adults who develop kyphosis can also wear braces, but, because their bones have stopped growing, the goal for them is mainly control of back pain.

Bowed legs often develop in children with skeletal dysplasias, especially after they start to walk. This is often made worse by too much weight gain adding pressure to the bones and joints. A few pounds of weight gain that may not show much on an average-sized person become very obvious on a person who is only 4 feet (1.22m) tall. For this reason, proper attention to diet along with moderate exercise is especially important. Loose joints or double-jointedness caused by lax ligaments is also a factor. "Many achondroplastic children can flex their finger, wrist, and knee joints to an abnormal degree because of ligament weakness," explains one specialist. "This also contributes to their bowleggedness."[30] If bowing becomes severe enough that the child's gait is affected, leg braces may be worn. The braces provide support and stability for the knee and may help the bowing from progressing. Braces are custom-built to fit each person's individual needs and are modified as the child grows.

Living with Disorders of Tall Stature

Being very tall can have its disadvantages as well. Very tall people have no trouble reaching things, but they do have problems fitting into spaces designed for average people. (One hotel in Chicago, recognizing this difficulty, has thirty-three "tall rooms," with longer beds and bathrobes and higher shower heads.) Doorways always present a problem; very tall people must frequently bend down so they do not bump their heads. Driving is difficult for tall people, too, because there is not enough legroom or headroom in an average car. Plane travel can be uncomfortable because of the lack of legroom. Many tall people pay extra for a first-class ticket just so they can fit into the seat space. Another disadvantage is that clothing has to be purchased from special stores or catalogs, often at a higher cost than the same items sized for average people.

People living with disorders of too much growth also have health issues. Regular medical checkups and maintaining a

Aquatic Therapy

Aquatic therapy, or AT, is a useful way to improve the physical limitations caused by skeletal dysplasias. Aquatic therapy is the use of specifically designed water activities by trained therapists to help restore, improve, and maintain the quality of muscle and joint function for people with disabilities. AT is usually supervised by a physical therapist, but physical therapy assistants, recreational therapists, or rehabilitation specialists can provide the therapy. AT provides many benefits, such as decreased pain from abnormal muscle tone, muscle spasms, and joint compression. It also increases mobility, range of motion of the joints, balance and coordination, posture, and muscle strength and endurance.

AT has certain advantages over regular physical therapy. First, the buoyancy of the water gives the individual extra support, allowing him or her to exercise without a lot of strain on the weight-bearing joints and allowing the muscles to move through a wider range of motion. Second, the pressure of the water on the body helps blood circulate from the legs to the heart, often reducing or preventing swelling in the ankles and feet. Third, on land, muscle-strengthening resistance comes from gravity, so muscle-strengthening resistance is felt in only one direction. In water, resistance is provided in every direction, promoting a more balanced muscle development. Fourth, the water in the pool is usually heated. Warm water relaxes muscles and reduces joint stiffness. "The warmth of the water establishes an environment of relaxation and peacefulness," says Andrea Poteat Salzman of the Aquatic Resources Network. "The patient is touched and touch by itself is often healing. Fluid movements are easier to perform than their counterparts on land. Joint mobilization, soft tissue elongation, and massage become less like therapy and more like dance."

From the home page of Aquatic Resources Network, www.aquaticnet.com/media.htm.

close working relationship with health-care providers are important aspects of living with both endocrine and genetic disorders such as acromegaly and Marfan syndrome.

People with acromegaly often have enlargement of the joints, causing painful arthritis. They may require surgical replacement of the painful joints, such as hip replacement. Thickened tissue in the hands and wrists can trap nerves, causing numbness and weakness in the hands. Surgery is necessary to release the entrapped nerves. Like people with achondroplasia, they may also have problems with sleep apnea. They can also have thickening

Yao Defeng, who suffers from acromegaly, is helped past a doorway at a hospital in Shanghai, China. She has numerous health problems, including high blood pressure, osteoporosis, and malnutrition, all due to an excess of growth hormones.

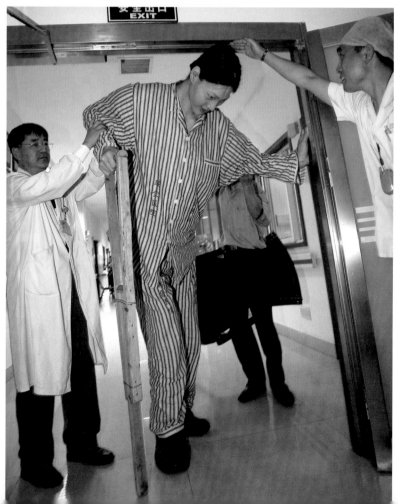

of the heart, causing shortness of breath, especially with exercise. They must be careful not to overexert themselves.

Marfan syndrome is another disorder of tall stature that has several related health problems. More than half of people with Marfan syndrome have dislocation of the lens of one or both eyes. Regular eye examinations are important for catching and correcting vision problems early. Usually, glasses or contact lenses can correct the problem. If the heart and blood vessels are involved, regular checkups help the doctor monitor the size of the aorta and make sure the heart valves are working.

Children diagnosed with Marfan syndrome must be careful when it comes to sports, since overexertion can put a lot of stress on the heart and blood vessels. They should avoid sports that involve a lot of running, excess strain on muscles, or the chance of getting hit, such as basketball, football, or track. They can participate in lots of other activities with their friends, though, like bike riding, swimming, or dancing. They just may need to go at a slower pace. As they get into their teens, some kids with Marfan syndrome may want to rebel against the disease that restricts them so much. They may even stop taking their heart medication. As one pediatric cardiologist says, "In my last twelve years I've seen two teenagers who came in with much larger aortas than the year before. In both cases the kids had stopped taking their medicine."[31]

Social Adaptations to Growth Disorders

Besides the medical aspects of these disorders, there are the obvious differences in appearance that can impact a person's self-esteem and outlook. People who look very different from what is considered normal must cope with stares, whispered comments, and thoughtless remarks and behavior. Bonnie, a teacher with achondroplasia, says: "I get tired of being stared at in the grocery store, in Wal-Mart, in a new town. People have asked me if I've been in the circus."[32] Ivy, an achondroplastic dwarf, says, "We look very different. Everywhere I go, I attract curiosity, and there are aspects of being a small person which are very difficult, but I would be the first person to disagree with the assumption that small people are in some way brave, special, or cute. We are normal people, living normal lives. We are born, eat, sleep, breathe, work, study, marry, have children, get ill, and die, just like everyone else."[33]

Children who are very short for any reason are often subjected to teasing and bullying by their peers. They are called all sorts of names, like Shorty or Shrimp. They are often rejected by other kids because they are considered too small to play the games other kids play. Adults tend to treat them as if they were much younger than they are and have lower expectations for them.

Although our society is more accepting of tall stature than of short stature, tall children, especially girls, also may get teased by their peers. They may feel awkward and clumsy. As tall girls start adolescence, they often worry about dating. Adults tend to expect more from tall children because they look older. Children and teens who have trouble accepting their height and dealing with these issues may need extra counseling and support to help them cope.

Economic Considerations

Growth disorders can also have an economic impact on people's lives. Short-statured adults can do almost any job that average-height people can do, but they may find job opportunities closed to them because of their appearance or their size, even if they are well qualified. Debra, who was born with a form of dwarfism that has not yet been diagnosed, experienced this after she graduated from college and tried to find a job. "Suddenly doors were being slammed in my face," she says. "They would tell me I'd give the company a bad image, and I'd be better off staying home. Or they'd tell me the position was filled, and I'd call back a few days later and it was still open. I'd say look, I have an education, I'm well read, just give me a chance, but they didn't understand." Eventually Debra did get a teaching job at an elementary school. "All the kids were my size," she says, "so it worked out really well."[34]

Research studies in short adults have linked short stature to problems with employment. In one such study, several hun-

A seven-year-old boy with Marfan syndrome sits out from basketball practice so his grandmother can put a chest guard on him to protect his heart. Children with Marfan syndrome must be very careful when playing sports.

dred college students were asked to rate certain qualities in men of different heights. Short men were rated as less mature, less positive, more insecure, less masculine, less successful, less capable, and less outgoing. Another study showed that when an employer was given resumes with the same qualifications, the taller man was hired seventy-five percent of the time. People in high-ranking jobs are, on average, 2 inches (5cm) taller than people in lower-status jobs, even if they have the same education and test scores. Studies have also shown that the taller a person is, the higher his or her average income.

Support and Encouragement

Having a growth disorder means looking very different from what is considered normal. Having a group to identify with and feel comfortable with is important for all people. Whether a person is "too short" or "too tall," people with growth disorders often feel set apart and isolated from the community around them. It can be difficult to keep a positive outlook and attitude about life in the face of blatant stares, rude comments and questions, and discrimination.

Joining a support group is one way to become involved with other people who face the same challenges. Support groups provide not only emotional support and companionship, but education and financial resources. When her son was born with dwarfism, Bonnie realized that they would need some kind of support network. A nurse at the hospital who had a relative with dwarfism encouraged her to contact the local chapter of Little People of America. Bonnie was glad she did. "When Stacy was born," she says, "I learned so many things I had avoided. I learned about precautions I had to take and things we are susceptible to." Besides learning about different health issues, she found a community of people who had been through many of the same experiences she had. She also felt it was important for her son to be around other kids like him. "I got moral support from people my age who were dealing with the same things,"[35] she says.

There are many support groups available for those with growth disorders. Among them are the Magic Foundation for Children's Growth, for families of children affected by short stature from any cause; the Human Growth Foundation, heavily involved in education and research; the National Marfan Foundation; and the Pituitary Network Association, founded in 1992 by a group of people with acromegaly. Many Web sites, such as Short Persons Support and Dwarfism.org, for example, offer a wide choice of products, services, and support sources for those living with growth disorders.

CHAPTER FIVE

On the Horizon

There are literally hundreds of different types of growth disorders. Some kinds of disorders have yet to be diagnosed and named, and some have so far been seen in only one individual. Genetic research, such as the Human Genome Project, focuses on discovering which genes are responsible for a particular disorder and on why genetic mutations cause the particular signs that they do. Research into endocrine growth disorders is centered on finding new applications for hormone replacement therapy and improving its effectiveness. Studies are also being done that look at the psychological, social, and economic impact of growth disorders.

The Human Genome Project

A major breakthrough in the understanding of genetic growth disorders occurred with the mapping of the human genome. A genome is the complete set of DNA in any living organism, plant or animal. An organism's genome includes all of its genes, containing the code, or blueprint, for the growth, development, appearance, and functioning of the organism. The human genome contains over 3 billion base pairs, or DNA units.

In 1990 scientists from the United States, the United Kingdom, France, Germany, Japan, and China began work on the Human Genome Project. The goal of the project was to map out the entire sequence of the twenty thousand to twenty-five thousand genes included in the human genome and identify them. The project was expected to take about fifteen years, but the work moved so quickly that it was completed in 2003, two years

A geneticist working for the Human Genome Project uses a sequencing machine.

ahead of schedule. Research continues worldwide, with several goals for the future that will have a direct impact on the early detection, diagnosis, treatment, and prevention of genetic diseases, including genetic growth disorders such as skeletal dysplasias and Marfan syndrome. For example, researchers are currently working with specially bred mice that carry the gene for Marfan syndrome in order to identify the specific mutations in the gene that cause Marfan syndrome. This will help to develop more accurate ways to diagnose the disorder. Understanding how each mutation actually changes the body's connective tissue and causes its symptoms will help doctors understand why people with Marfan syndrome are affected differently and will hopefully lead to more effective treatments.

Genes and Pituitary Tumors

Scientists are also using the information gathered from genetic research to learn more about pituitary tumors in children. Researchers at the National Institute of Child Health and Human Development are currently analyzing data from a study that ended in January 2006. One of the goals of the study was to identify genetic factors that may make a child more likely to develop a pituitary tumor. They studied the inheritance patterns of pituitary tumors and their possible connection with other conditions in the families of the children with the tumors. They also examined the genetics of actual tumor tissue. They hope that the information learned from this research will lead to the development of better ways to treat pituitary tumors in children.

Genetic Research on Achondroplasia

In 1994 researchers identified the exact gene, as well as the specific mutation on the gene, that causes achondroplasia. This discovery made it possible to develop highly accurate tests that could confirm or rule out a diagnosis of achondroplasia before birth. The gene is one of a group of genes called fibroblast growth factor receptors. It controls the production of a protein that is located on the surface of cartilage cells. The

Scientists are using information from genetic research to learn more about brain tumors in children.

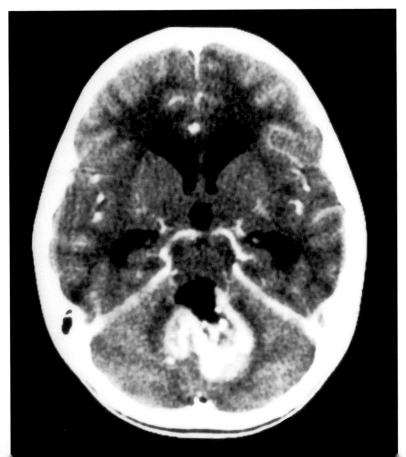

achondroplasia mutation interferes with the way the protein on the cartilage cells responds to growth factors that stimulate them to grow. Scientists are studying how the faulty protein actually causes the distinct features of achondroplasia. The hope is that this information will lead to better treatments for the disorder, as well as for other skeletal dysplasias.

Gene Therapy

Another way to apply the knowledge gained from the Human Genome Project is in the area of gene therapy. Also called genetic engineering, gene therapy involves introducing normal genes into targeted cells that are adversely affected by an abnormal gene.

There are two forms of gene therapy. In somatic gene therapy, the normal gene is introduced into the targeted cells so that they receive the correct information about what they are supposed to do. This form of gene therapy treats the patient, but not his or her children, since the new gene is not passed on. This is the more common kind of gene therapy, and it has been used since 1990 to treat such diseases as severe immune deficiency. As of 2000 more than 250 somatic gene therapy trials were underway. The most promising use so far will be to treat single gene defects that cause significant disabilities and cannot be treated any other way.

The other form of gene therapy is called germ line gene therapy. This method actually changes the genes in the sperm or egg cell, so that the new gene is passed down to future generations. Experiments with this kind of gene therapy involved injecting fragments of DNA into fertilized mouse egg cells. The treated mice grew to adulthood and gave birth to offspring that also had the new DNA in their cells. Scientists discovered that certain growth problems in mice could be corrected this way. The concept of altering human reproductive cells is extremely controversial, however, and to date, research in this area has been limited both for technical and ethical reasons. Although the use of gene therapy for growth disorders is still far in the future, scientists hope that someday the technology will be perfected

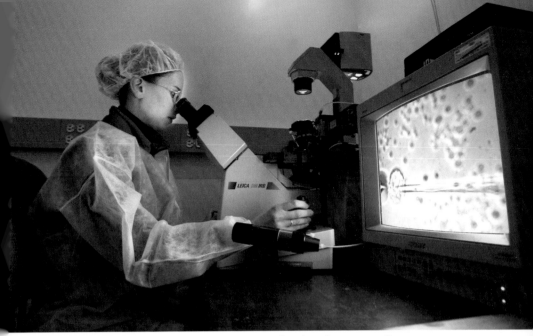
A scientist microinjects DNA into fertilized mouse cells.

enough that it will become a safe and acceptable way to treat and prevent certain growth disorders.

Genes and Growth Hormone

While gene therapy has had only limited attention for the treatment of growth disorders, genetic technology has had a significant impact on growth disorders in the area of growth hormone treatment. By the 1950s scientists understood the relationship of growth hormone to short stature. In the late 1950s a scientist named Maurice Raben had purified enough growth hormone from human pituitary glands to treat a boy with growth hormone deficiency. The use of growth hormone for this purpose slowly became more widespread. At that time, however, the only source of human growth hormone was the pituitary glands of cadavers. Supplies were limited, and only the most severely affected children were treated. A potential danger of the new treatment arose when it was discovered that a fatal viral disease of the brain called Creutzfeldt-Jakob disease could possibly be transmitted this way. After the purification process was improved, the shortage worsened as more and more physicians wanted to treat their shortest patients with growth hormone.

In 1981 a new American company called Genentech started trials with synthetic, or man-made, growth hormone, using a new technology called recombinant DNA technology. In this technology, human genes for growth hormone production were inserted into bacteria so that huge amounts of the hormone would be made by the bacteria. Like any new technology, long safety trials were conducted over the next several years.

Meanwhile in 1985, four young adults who had received cadaver growth hormone in the 1960s developed the fatal Creutzfeldt-Jakob disease. The use of this source of growth hormone quickly came to an end. Approval of the synthetic hormone by the Food and Drug Administration (FDA) came soon after that, and in late 1985 Protropin was introduced in the United States. Within a few years, other companies in the United States and Europe began marketing their own brands of synthetic growth hormone. Treatment was limited to only those children whose shortness was due to a deficiency of growth hormone. By the mid-1990s, however, the FDA had approved the use of growth hormone to treat short stature from other causes, such as achondroplasia, Turner syndrome, inflammatory bowel diseases, or long-term kidney failure. In 1999 the FDA approved a new, long-acting form of growth hormone for children with growth hormone deficiency. This form of synthetic, or artificial, growth hormone requires injections only once or twice a month instead of every day. Studies are also underway to evaluate the safety and effectiveness of a form of growth hormone that can be inhaled, rather than injected.

Looking More Closely at Growth Hormone

Now that growth hormone is readily available and has been approved for a wide range of height problems, scientists are looking more closely at how growth hormone treatment interacts with other variables that affect growth. In April 2006 scientists at the University of Alabama in Birmingham began a study that will evaluate the effect growth hormone has on phosphorus levels in the body. Phosphorus is an important mineral necessary for bone growth. Phosphorus levels are controlled by the kidneys with the help of a substance called fibroblast growth factor 23. The study will look at how growth hormone affects the action of fibroblast 23.

Researchers at Nemours Clinic in Jacksonville, Florida, are currently looking at the relationship between growth hormone and energy consumption in boys. This study began in May 2004. Two groups of boys, seven to ten years old, who were very short and below average in weight, were studied. The first group was simply observed for the first six months, then received injections of growth hormone for the next twelve months. The other group received a high-calorie drink every day for the first six months, then received growth hormone injections plus the drink for the next twelve months. The boys' changes in height, weight, and body composition are being compared to see if the high-calorie drink made a difference in the effect of the hormone injections.

Looking at Other Hormones

In 2005 researchers at the University of California–Los Angeles (UCLA) presented data that showed that as many as thirty thousand children in the United States who are very short may have a deficiency of insulin-like growth factor (IGF-1), even though their growth hormone level is normal. This is called primary IGFD. The UCLA study looked at 4,663 children who had been diagnosed with short stature due to hormone deficiency. The study found that primary IGFD was about as frequent as short stature caused by growth hormone deficiency. Also in 2005, the FDA approved two new drugs for the treatment of primary IGFD. "In the future," says one of the researchers, "studies should determine how the new diagnostic entity of IGFD should be approached with the expanding array of growth-promoting therapeutic agents and strategies."[36]

One such study is currently underway at forty medical centers across the United States. The study began in May 2005 and is following 160 children. Children in the study will receive synthetic IGF-1, which is identical to the naturally produced hormone. "This is the first new prospective treatment in thirty years to pro-

Recombinant DNA Technology

Recombinant DNA begins with the identification of a gene that carries the code for a desired protein. The desired protein might be insulin, a vaccine, growth hormone, or some other protein. Substances called restriction enzymes are used to cut the desired part of the DNA and insert it into a vector. A vector is a piece of DNA found in some bacteria and viruses that can grow and divide by itself. In this way, two pieces of DNA that do not naturally occur together are recombined. Once the desired DNA is inserted into the vector, it is cloned. Cloning is necessary to produce many copies of the recombined DNA.

Once the vector has been cloned it is introduced into host cells such as yeast or bacteria. The host cells will then respond to the new recombinant DNA by producing the desired protein. The protein can then be isolated and purified in large amounts.

Recombinant DNA technology was first discovered in 1973 and was made possible by the discovery of restriction enzymes. Because of recombinant technology physicians no longer have to rely on biological sources such as cadaver pituitary tissue, which are not as pure and can carry disease.

vide an alternative therapy for short stature," says Dr. Michael Gottschalk, professor of pediatrics at the University of California–San Diego, one of the centers participating in the study. "Traditionally, physicians have used growth hormone replacement to raise levels and improve growth rates. However, there are many short stature children who are not deficient in growth hormone, but there is no known cause for their disease."[37]

A similar study is also underway at Rush University Medical Center in Chicago. According to Dr. Richard Levy, a pediatric endocrinologist at Rush: "Patients who are deficient in IGF-1 and resistant to the effects of growth hormone do not respond well, if at all, to the shots. Instead of using growth hormone to stimulate the production of IGF-1, the goal is to replace the IGF-1 directly."[38]

In another study at UCLA presented in 2005, scientists used their knowledge of the relationship between growth hormone and IGF-1 to improve height outcomes in children with growth hormone deficiency and with idiopathic short stature. Traditionally, growth hormone dosages were based only on the weight of the child—the heavier the child, the higher the dosage. This study looked at basing the dose on how growth hormone affects IGF-1 levels, rather than on weight. Researchers divided the children into three groups. One group received traditional doses of growth hormone based on weight. Another group received doses of growth hormone aimed at achieving a normal level of IGF-1 for their age and gender. The third group received growth hormone at doses designed to achieve a high level of IGF-1. The study showed that children in the third group grew 50 percent better than the children in the other two groups. The result was the same whether the children had growth hormone deficiency or idiopathic short stature.

This was an important discovery, because there is a great deal of variation in how different children respond to their doses of growth hormone. The researchers who conducted the study feel that this new way of dosing will provide a much more fine-tuned method of dosing, making it both safer and more effective. In the second phase of this research completed in July 2006, the researchers applied their new dosing strategy to a group of approximately one hundred prepubertal children currently being treated with growth hormone. When all the data have been analyzed, they hope to confirm that the dosing method based on IGF-1 levels is in fact safer and more effective than weight-based dosing.

New Hope for Marfan Syndrome

In addition to research into the genetic aspects of Marfan syndrome, scientists are discovering new ways to treat the features of the disorder using both medications and surgical methods. Early in 2006 scientists at Johns Hopkins University

discovered that a medication called losartan, a commonly prescribed blood pressure medication, helps to prevent the most
dangerous complication of Marfan syndrome—the weakening
of the wall of the aorta, the largest artery in the body. This
weakening, called an aneurysm, can cause the aorta to widen
over time and eventually rupture like an overfilled balloon,
causing life-threatening loss of blood. Another serious complication is called an aortic dissection. This occurs when the in-
nermost layer of the aorta, called the intima, tears, allowing
blood to leak into the space between the layers and causing the
layers to separate from one another. Both aneurysms and dissections are potentially life-threatening events.

Earlier research had shown that some of the symptoms of
Marfan syndrome are related to increased activity of a molecule called TGFbeta. Scientists had already demonstrated that
blocking the activity of this molecule in specially bred mice
with the Marfan gene could prevent serious lung disease in the
mice. It also improved diseased heart valves and weakened
aortas in the mice. "The real problem," says Dr. Hal Dietz of
Johns Hopkins, "was that the methods we had used to block
TGFbeta could not be easily applied to humans."[39]

The researchers turned their attention to losartan. "This was
an attractive choice," says Dr. Dietz, "because losartan lowers
blood pressure, something known to be good for people with
aortic aneurysms; it is already approved by the FDA for the
treatment of hypertension [high blood pressure] in adults, and
has been shown both in people and in animal models to decrease TGFbeta signaling."[40] A trial in mice was begun. After
nine months of treatment with losartan, the aortas in the
treated mice were entirely normal and no different from those
in mice that did not have the Marfan gene. "It is very exciting
that an existing medication has proven capable of not only
treating the problems of Marfan syndrome, but also disrupting
the biological pathway that precipitated them,"[41] says geneticist Daniel P. Judge of Hopkins. Heart surgeon Vincent Gott,
who is a pioneer in the surgical repair of aortic aneurysms in
Marfan patients, says, "Until now, surgery has been our main

A Better Fix for Marfan Patients

Aortic aneurysms and dissections are the most serious complications faced by people with Marfan syndrome. Traditional surgical methods to repair these problems have involved opening the chest or the abdomen and replacing the affected part of the vessel with an artificial graft. This kind of surgery carries a great deal of risk for the patient. The aorta must be clamped off while it is being replaced, interrupting the blood supply to the rest of the body. There can be a great deal of blood loss during the surgery. Patients must spend some time in the intensive care unit after surgery, often on a ventilator.

A newer way of repairing aneurysms and dissections is called endovascular stent graft repair. First introduced in 1991, this surgery involves making a small incision in each groin to get to the femoral arteries. A long, narrow device containing a collapsed aortic graft is passed into the femoral arteries and up into the aorta until it arrives at the weakened area. The device is then removed and the graft remains behind, expanding to fit inside the aorta. This allows blood to flow through the graft without putting high pressure on the weak aorta.

This kind of repair is less risky to the patient because it does not require a large incision in the chest or abdomen. The aorta does not have to be clamped off. There is much less loss of blood and less need for blood transfusions. Patients often do not need to go to the intensive care unit afterward, and they can go home much sooner than after a traditional repair.

option for repairing an aorta at risk of rupturing. However, it is comforting to witness the time when medication could prevent this disease, making surgery unnecessary."[42]

Developments in Surgery

Another serious complication of Marfan syndrome that affects both the heart and the aorta is weakening of the portion of the aorta that joins the heart. This part of the aorta, along with the heart valve just below it, is called the aortic root. Arising from the left ventricle of the heart, the aortic root bears the high pressures of every heartbeat, so it is particularly vulnerable to weakening in Marfan patients. Traditionally, surgery to fix this part of the aorta has also included replacing the valve attached to it with an artificial one. Because blood clots can form on the artificial valve, patients have to take an anticoagulant, or blood-thinning medication, for the rest of their lives. This increases their risk of bleeding, however, and requires blood tests every month to make sure the drug level is right.

For the last ten years a newer operation has been available that does not replace the valve but leaves it intact, replacing only the portion of the aorta coming off of it. This surgery, called aortic valve-sparing surgery, is more difficult to perform, but it eliminates the need for the anticoagulant. "Valve-sparing surgery takes two hours longer than a total replacement,"[43] says one surgeon, adding that almost all of his younger patients choose to have the valve-sparing surgery.

To help Marfan patients faced with this decision, researchers from all over the world are currently working together on a study sponsored by the National Marfan Foundation that will help establish which type of surgery is better for Marfan patients. The study will also provide more information about how aortic disease occurs in people with Marfan syndrome.

Millions of people worldwide are affected by some kind of growth disorder or height issue. Growth disorders have been misunderstood by society, largely because of fairy tales and legends about giants and dwarfs. In modern times the entertainment industry has perpetuated this misunderstanding. Fortunately, with advances in medicine and technology along with increased awareness and acceptance of those affected, people living with growth disorders have a brighter future ahead.

Notes

Introduction: The Importance of Height

1. Quoted in Peggy Peck, "Growth Hormone Helps Short Children Achieve Normal Height," *Medscape Medical News*, October 13, 2004.
2. Ivy Broadhead, "Living with Achondroplasia," *Evening Chronicle*, August 4, 2005. http://icnewcastle.icnetwork. co.uk/eveningchronicle/features/tm_objectid=1581536& method=full&siteid=50081&headline=it-s-a-tall-world-for-people-like-me-name_page.html.
3. Ivy Broadhead, "Living with Achondroplasia."
4. Quoted in Susan Carlton, "Short Stuff," *Parenting*, November 2001, p. 196.
5. Quoted in *Time for Kids*, "A Short and Sweet Study," September 17, 2004, p. 3.

Chapter One: What Are Growth Disorders?

6. Louise Duncombe, "My Experiences as a Female," Short Support, May 2005. www.shortsupport.org.
7. Dina, interview with author, Springfield, Missouri, October 5, 2006.
8. Quoted in Tresa McBee, "Cameron's Got Charm," *Springfield* (MO) *News-Leader*, December 18, 2005, p. 1C.
9. Kate Gilbert Phifer, *Growing Up Small: A Handbook for Short People*. Middlebury, VT: Paul S. Erickson, 1979, p. 35.
10. Quoted in Medical News Today, "Study Concludes Primary IGF-1 Deficiency Is a Frequent Cause of Short Stature," by Mechal Weiss. May 17, 2005. www.medicalnewstoday.com/medicalnews.php?newsid=24493.

Chapter Two: Diagnosing Growth Disorders

11. Dina, interview.
12. Quoted in Randi Henderson and Marjorie Centofani, "Life as a Little Person," *Hopkins Medical News*, Spring/Summer, 1995.

13. Quoted in J.D. Heyman et al., "Drugs Can Make Short Kids Grow, but Is It Right to Prescribe Them?" *People*, September 15, 2003, pp. 103–104.
14. Quoted in Vincent Ianelli, "Short Children," About.com, November 26, 2003. http://pediatrics.about.com/cs/weekly question/a/040302_ask.htm.
15. Quoted in Krista Conger, "Heartfelt Help: Stanford Caregivers Thwart Marfan Syndrome's Deadly Course," *Stanford Medicine*, Summer 2003. http://mednews.stanford. edu/stanmed/2003Summer/heartfelt.html.
16. Quoted in Jennifer M. Phelps, "Acromegaly Linked to Growth Hormone," *Springfield* (MO) *News-Leader*, June 13, 2006.
17. Dina, interview.

Chapter Three: Treating Growth Disorders

18. Quoted in Doctor's Guide to Medical and Other News, "Geref Products Launched for Diagnosis and Treatment of Growth Problems," 1999. www.docguide.com.
19. Quoted in Arlene Weintraub and Michael Arndt, "My How You've Grown," *Business Week*, November 28, 2005, pp. 86–88.
20. Quoted in Special Child: Disorder Zone Archives, "Hydrocephalus." www.specialchild.com/disorder.html.
21. Quoted in Henderson and Centofani, "Life as a Little Person."
22. Quoted in Henderson and Centofani, "Life as a Little Person."

Chapter Four: Living with Growth Disorders

23. Dina, interview.
24. Cameron, interview with author, Springfield, Missouri, October 5, 2006.
25. Willem Winkelman and Rachel Buchholz, "Keep Staring: I Might Do a Trick," *National Geographic Kids*, November 2004, pp. 46–48.
26. Dina, interview.
27. Quoted in Henderson and Centofani, "Life as a Little Person."

28. Phifer, *Growing Up Small*, p. 146.
29. Quoted in Henderson and Centofani, "Life as a Little Person."
30. Phifer, *Growing Up Small*, p. 147.
31. Quoted in Conger, "Heartfelt Help."
32. Quoted in Carrie Ferguson, "A Lesson in Perseverance," *Tennessean*, June 17, 2001. www.Tennessean.com/local/archives.
33. Ivy Broadhead, "Living with Achondroplasia."
34. Quoted in Sam Boykin, "Standing Tall—Little People Making It in a Big World," *Creative Loafing Charlotte*, January 12, 2002. http://charlotte.creativeloafing.com/gyrobase/Content?oid=oid%3A592.
35. Quoted in Ferguson, "A Lesson in Perseverance."

Chapter Five: On the Horizon

36. Quoted in Medical News Today, "Study Concludes Primary IGF-1 Deficiency Is a Frequent Cause of Short Stature."
37. Quoted in UCSD Medical Center, "UCSD Medical Center and Children's Hospital to Participate in Clinical Study for Short Stature," news release, May 16, 2005. http://health.ucsd.edu/news/2005/05_16_Study.htm.
38. Quoted in Rush University Medical Center, "Study of New Treatment for Short Stature Underway at Rush University Medical Center," news release, September 20, 2005. www.sciencedaily.com/print.php?url=releases/2005/09/050920081239.htm.
39. Hal Dietz, "A Whole Lot of Optimism (Tempered by a Healthy Dose of Caution)," National Marfan Foundation, 2006. www.marfan.org.
40. Dietz, "A Whole Lot of Optimism."
41. Quoted in Johns Hopkins Medicine, "Commonly Used Blood Pressure Medication Prevents Aortic Aneurysm in Mice with Marfan Syndrome, Hopkins Study Shows," news release, April 6, 2006. www.hopkinsmedicine.org.
42. Quoted in Johns Hopkins Medicine, "Commonly Prescribed Blood Pressure Medicine Prevents Aortic Aneurysm in Mice with Marfan Syndrome."
43. Quoted in Conger, "Hertfelt Help."

Glossary

achondroplasia: A genetic growth disorder causing abnormal cartilage production at the ends of the long bones, characterized by shortened limbs, a large head, and average-sized torso.

acromegaly: A growth disorder caused by overproduction of growth hormone after growth has stopped.

ACTH: Adrenocorticotropic hormone. Produced by the pituitary, it controls the production of cortisol by the adrenal glands.

adrenal glands: Small endocrine glands located just above each kidney. They produce the hormones cortisol and adrenaline.

amniocentesis: A diagnostic test in which amniotic fluid is withdrawn from the uterus during pregnancy and the cells in it are examined for genetic abnormalities.

amniotic fluid: The fluid that surrounds the fetus in the uterus.

biliary atresia: A liver disease in which the tiny tubes that carry bile out of the liver are blocked or malformed. It causes severe damage to the liver and is usually treatable only with a liver transplant.

bone age: A measure of the skeletal development of a child or teen.

bone age X-ray: An X-ray of the hand that compares a child's bone age with his or her chronological age.

cartilage: Tough, elastic connective tissue found at the ends of the bones and in the ear, nose, and larynx.

celiac disease: A digestive disorder in which the body cannot metabolize gluten, a protein found in many grains, especially wheat. It prevents proper absorption of nutrients and can lead to growth failure. Treatment involves changes in diet.

chorionic villi: Threadlike strands of tissue that form part of the placenta.

chorionic villus sampling: A diagnostic test in which a small piece of chorionic villi is removed during pregnancy and tested for genetic abnormalities.

chromosomes: Threadlike structures located in the nucleus of most living cells that carry the genes.

constitutional growth delay: A normal variation of growth in which growth slows in early childhood. Puberty is often delayed, allowing a period of catch-up growth in the teens.

craniopharyngioma: A benign tumor of the brain, commonly seen in children, that can press on the pituitary or hypothalamus and cause them to malfunction.

Crohn's disease: A disease in which the small intestine becomes inflamed and may develop ulcers. It causes abdominal pain and rapid emptying of the intestine, interfering with absorption of nutrients from food. Treatment involves medications and often surgery.

Cushing's syndrome: An endocrine disorder caused by an overproduction of cortisol, leading to growth retardation.

disproportionate dwarfism: A form of dwarfism in which the limbs are much shorter in proportion to the rest of the body.

DNA: Deoxyribonucleic acid. The substance that makes up the chemical composition of genes.

dominant gene: A gene that requires only one copy to be inherited in order for its characteristic to show.

dwarfism: Any condition that results in an adult height of less than 4 feet 10 inches (1.47m).

encephalitis: An inflammation of the brain caused by infections.

endocrine glands: Small organs located throughout the body that are responsible for secreting various hormones that control many aspects of growth and reproduction.

endocrinology: The branch of science and medicine that deals with endocrine disorders.

familial short stature: A variation of growth in which a person's short stature is a result of inheritance from his or her parents.

gene: A unit of DNA, located on a chromosome, that carries the code for a specific characteristic.

genetic testing: Diagnostic tests that examine the DNA of cells to detect the presence of genetic abnormalities.

genome: The entire sequence of DNA for an organism.

gigantism: A rare growth disorder caused by an overproduction of growth hormone during childhood, resulting in extremely tall stature.

growth chart: A chart used by physicians to track the growth pattern of a child or teen.

growth hormone deficiency: An underproduction of growth hormone caused by various problems with the pituitary, resulting in abnormally short stature.

growth hormone stimulation test: Also called an arginine test, in which the amino acid arginine is injected to stimulate the release of growth hormone by the pituitary.

growth plates: Specialized structures at the ends of the long bones in children that manufacture bone cells and are responsible for bone growth. At puberty, the growth plates fuse to the bones and growth stops.

heredity: The characteristics inherited from one's ancestors, especially parents.

hormone: A chemical produced by an endocrine gland that sends instructions to specific target cells, telling them what to do.

hydrocephalus: An abnormal collection of fluid on the brain, commonly seen in children with achondroplasia.

hypopituitarism: An endocrine disorder in which the pituitary gland fails to produce adequate amounts of its hormones.

hypothalamus: The region of the brain that controls sleep cycles, appetite, and body temperature and acts as an endocrine gland by producing hormones that regulate the activities of the pituitary.

hypothyroidism: An endocrine disorder that causes an underproduction of thyroid hormone, leading to growth retardation. In newborns, it can cause severe mental retardation if untreated.

idiopathic: A medical term meaning "of unknown cause."

insulin-like growth factor 1 (IGF-1): A hormone produced in the liver and other organs in response to growth hormone, which is necessary for normal growth.

kyphosis: Abnormal outward curvature of the upper spine, causing a humpbacked appearance.

lordosis: An abnormal inward curvature of the lower spine, causing a swaybacked appearance.

Marfan syndrome: A genetic disorder of the body's connective tissue that causes tall stature, joint instability, and vascular and eye abnormalities.

meningitis: Inflammation of the meninges, the tissues surrounding the brain and spinal cord.

mutation: A change in the DNA of a gene, which may or may not cause a health problem.

neonatal hepatitis: Inflammation of the liver that occurs in infants, usually between one and two months after birth. It can damage the liver and may require a liver transplant.

osteogenesis imperfecta: A genetic disorder that causes brittle bones.

pituitary adenoma: A usually benign tumor of the pituitary that may or may not secrete hormones.

pituitary gland: A pea-sized gland located at the base of the brain that secretes hormones that control all hormonal functions of the body. Often called the master gland.

proportionate dwarfism: A form of short stature in which the body parts are in normal proportion to each other.

psychogenic dwarfism: A condition of growth retardation caused by long-term neglect and abuse.

puberty: The stage of growth during which adult sexual characteristics appear and growth stops.

recessive gene: A gene that requires both copies to be inherited in order for its characteristic to show.

serum albumin level: A measurement of the amount of the protein albumin in the blood. It helps indicate how well a person is nourished.

skeletal dysplasia: The term for any disorder of growth that involves abnormal development of the bones.

skeletal survey: An X-ray of the entire skeleton, used for detecting abnormalities of the skeleton.

sleep apnea: A temporary interruption in breathing during sleep caused by obstruction of the upper airway.

sonogram: The image created by reflected sound waves during an ultrasound exam.

spinal stenosis: Narrowing of the spinal canal, causing pressure on the spinal cord.

thyroid gland: A butterfly-shaped endocrine gland located at the base of the throat that produces thyroid hormones.

thyroid-stimulating hormone: Produced by the pituitary, it controls the production of thyroid hormones by the thyroid gland.

tracheotomy: A surgically created opening in the trachea, or windpipe, that allows a person with a blocked upper airway to breathe.

Turner syndrome: A genetic disorder in girls in which all or part of an X chromosome is missing, resulting in underdeveloped ovaries and short stature.

ultrasound: A diagnostic test in which ultrasonic or very high frequency sound waves are used to create an image of an unborn baby or internal organs.

Organizations to Contact

Aquatic Resources Network
3500 Vicksburg La. N., #250
Plymouth, MN 55447
(715) 248-7258
Web site: www.aquaticnet.com
e-mail: info@aquaticnet.com

This organization provides membership information, educational resources, and product information related to aquatic therapy.

The Hormone Foundation
8401 Connecticut Ave., Suite 900
Chevy Chase, MD 20815-5817
(800) HORMONE
Web site: www.hormone.org
e-mail: hormone@endo-society.org

Dedicated to serving as a resource for the public by promoting the prevention, treatment, and cure of hormone-related conditions through public outreach and education.

Human Growth Foundation
997 Glen Cove Ave.
Glen Head, NY 11545
(800) 451-6434
Web site: www.hgfound.org
e-mail: hgfl@hgfound.org

A nonprofit national organization of families with short children and others interested in growth problems. Its goals are research support, parent education, and education of the public and the health-care professions.

Little People of America National Headquarters

PO Box 9897
Washington, DC 20016
(888) LPA-2001
Web site: www.lpaonline.org
e-mail: info@lpaonline.org

Provides peer support along with social and educational opportunities to individuals with dwarfism and their families,
along with education for the public and medical community.

The MAGIC Foundation

6645 W. North Ave.
Oak Park, IL 60302
(800) 3MAGIC3
Web site: www.magicfoundation.org
e-mail: mary@magicfoundation.org

One of the largest support organizations in the United States for
families of children affected by short stature from any cause.

The National Marfan Foundation

22 Manhasset Ave.
Port Washington, NY 11050
(800) 8MARFAN
Web site: www.marfan.org
e-mail: staff@marfan.org

Dedicated to saving lives and improving the quality of life for
individuals and families of those affected by Marfan syndrome
and related disorders.

The Pituitary Network Association

PO Box 1958
Thousand Oaks, CA 91358
(805) 499-9973
Web site: www.pituitary.org
e-mail: PNA@pituitary.org

An international organization for patients with pituitary tumors and disorders, their families, loved ones, and physicians and health-care providers who treat them.

Turner Syndrome Society

14450 T.C. Jester, Suite 260
Houston, TX 77014
(800) 365-9944
Web site: www.turner-syndrome-us.org
e-mail: tssus@turner-syndrome-us.org

The Turner Syndrome Society provides support, education, and resources for girls and women with Turner syndrome, as well as their friends, families, doctors, and the public.

For Further Reading

Books

Lesli J. Favor, *Everything You Need to Know About Growth Spurts and Delayed Growth.* New York: Rosen, 2002. Outlines routine physical and emotional changes that are typical of any period of adolescence for both male and female children.

James W. Fiscus, *Coping with Growth Spurts and Delayed Growth.* New York: Rosen, 2002. Explores the physical growth that occurs in adolescence, physical and emotional difficulties that can accompany growth spurts, and rare but serious growth-related medical conditions that can occur.

Susan Kuklin, *Thinking Big: The Story of a Young Dwarf.* New York: Lothrop, Lee, and Shepard, 1986. The story of eight-year-old Jaime, who has achondroplasia. Good for younger readers.

Elaine Landau, *Short Stature: From Folklore to Fact.* New York: Franklin Watts, 1997. Presents historical and modern people with dwarfism, medical causes and treatments, and questions, concerns, and challenges for young people and adults living with this difference.

———, *Standing Tall: Unusually Tall People.* New York: Franklin Watts, 1997. Traces the treatment of giants throughout folklore, the challenges faced by unusually tall people, the medical reasons for gigantism and acromegaly, and the prejudices faced by tall people.

Kate Gilbert Phifer, *Tall and Small: A Book About Height.* New York: Walker, 1987. A useful book that explains why some of us are short and others are tall, with reassurance for those who may be concerned about their height.

Stephanie Riggs, *Never Sell Yourself Short.* Morton Grove, IL: Whitman, 2001. Fourteen-year-old Josh shows what his life is like as a dwarf. Good for younger readers.

Web Sites

Dwarfism.org (www.dwarfism.org). The goal of this Web site is to foster an online community of individuals interested in and/or affected by dwarfism and to provide a hub for the exchange of related information.

KidsHealth (www.kidshealth.org). Provides health information for kids, teens, and parents on a wide variety of health topics from before birth through adolescence.

MedlinePlus (medlineplus.gov). Brings together medical information from the National Library of Medicine, the National Institutes of Health, and other government agencies and health-related organizations.

Short Persons Support (www.shortsupport.org). Offers a variety of information related to short stature, with dozens of links to a wide variety of news articles, personal essays, and research news.

Videos

Big Enough. Directed by Jan Krawitz. Boston, MA: Fanlight Productions, 2004. A sequel to the video *Little People*.

Eye Level with America's Little People. Directed by Jeff Herring, Armando Koghan, and Dan McKinney, 2000. A documentary of the 1998 Little People of America national conference in Los Angeles.

Little People. Produced, directed, and edited by Jan Krawitz and Thomas Ott. Stanford University, Stanford, CA, 1984. This upbeat, award-winning film depicts the daily lives and struggles of little people in America and shows how attitudes about dwarfism are changing.

Index

About the Author

Lizabeth Peak received her bachelor of science in nursing from the University of Florida in 1978 and her bachelor of science in secondary education from Southwest Missouri State University in 1991. She currently works full-time as a surgical nurse, specializing in general and vascular surgery.

Lizabeth has published both fiction and nonfiction for adults and children. She especially enjoys writing about history, biography, and medical topics. She lives in Springfield, Missouri, with her husband, Brian, daughters Rebecca and Wendy, three dogs, and two cats. When she is not working or writing, she enjoys hiking, reading, and Saint Louis Cardinals baseball.